ALSO BY JOHN HERSEY

My Petition for More Space (1974)

The Writer's Craft (1974)

The Conspiracy (1972)

Letter to the Alumni (1970)

The Algiers Motel Incident (1968)

Under the Eye of the Storm (1967)

Too Far to Walk (1966)

White Lotus (1965)

Here to Stay (1963)

The Child Buyer (1960)

The War Lover (1959)

A Single Pebble (1956)

The Marmot Drive (1953)

The Wall (1950)

Hiroshima (1946)

A Bell for Adano (1944)

Into the Valley (1943)

THESE ARE BORZOI BOOKS
PUBLISHED IN NEW YORK BY ALFRED A. KNOPF

THE
PRESIDENT

THE
PRESIDENT

JOHN HERSEY

Alfred A. Knopf New York

1975

This material first appeared in *The New York Times
Magazine* April 20, 1975

"Send the Girls Over There," which appears on page
129, words and music by Richard M. Sherman &
Milton P. Larsen; from the record Album "Smash
Flops/Sing a Song of Sickness," produced by Oliver
Berliner; Copyright 1960 by Hall of Fame Music
Co., assigned to Annandale Music Co. All Rights
Reserved. Used by permission.

Library of Congress Number: 75–13675
ISBN: 0–394–45986–5   0–394–73148–4 (pbk.)

Manufactured in the United States of America
First Edition

Photographs by George Tames
Front-cover photograph by George Tames

FOR BARBARA

INTRODUCTION

AT HIS SWEARING-IN as President, in the East Room of the White House shortly after noon on August 9, 1974, Gerald Ford said, "I believe that truth is the glue that holds government together, not only our government but civilization itself. . . . In all my public and private acts as your President, I expect to follow my instincts of openness and candor with full confidence that honesty is always the best policy in the end. My fellow Americans, our long national nightmare is over. Our Constitution works; our great Republic is a government of laws and not of men. . . ." And introducing his first Press Secretary, Jerald terHorst, to the White House reporters less than an hour later, the new President repeated his promise: "We will have an open, we will have a candid administration. . . ."

After what had seemed the interminable agony of Richard Nixon's dissembling and withholding and tampering with the truth, Ford's declaration of intent to offer the nation an open administration was received with universal relief and hope. The very next day, *The New York Times'* Assistant Sunday Editor, Jack Rosenthal, a former Washington reporter, called his old friend terHorst to test this intent. He pointed out that Mr. Ford, the first unelected President of the United States, not having endured the grueling exposure of an electoral campaign, was little known to the public, and he asked terHorst to see whether the President would allow a writer extensive access to him over a period of days, for the gathering of material for a large portrait. TerHorst, while encouraging Rosenthal, asked for a bit of time for the new administration to settle into stride.

The administration's shakedown—and the national euphoria—lasted exactly a month: on September 8 came the Nixon pardon. It had been arranged in secret, with no consultation outside the White House, and with no preparation of the public mind, and the American people's elated sense of new beginnings came tumbling down—and, with it, some part of their confidence in Mr. Ford's "instincts of openness and candor." And on that day Jerald terHorst resigned in protest.

Shortly afterward, Rosenthal renewed his inquiry with the new Press Secretary, Ronald Nessen. It was December before the two men met. Having consulted with the President, Nessen then agreed in principle to the *Times'* proposal; he stipulated, however, that once the *Times* had assigned a writer, the President would have to meet him for "a sizing-up session" before the granting of final approval and before agreement on exact ground rules for the project.

On February 7, 1975, having been nominated for the assignment by the *Times*, I met with Mr. Ford and asked if I might follow him closely through a working week, and he replied at once that I might. When he asked what sorts of meetings I would like to sit in on, I said, "All of them. Everything." He saw no difficulty in that, he said; then he did quickly specify one exclusion, the full import of which did not strike me until late in the week of my visitation, as you will discover if you stay with Mr. Ford and me in these pages as far as Friday: he excepted "my daily meetings with Henry."

We then agreed that it would be best to make an arbitrary choice of a week at random, and to take our chances on whatever might happen during it, rather than to try to pick a week in which "special" occurrences might be foreseen; the events of the week would not in any case be news but only the backdrop against which the President's ways of being and doing would be displayed. Neither the President nor his Press Secretary asked to review any part of what I might write.

The week of my visit, in the event, was the one beginning Monday, March 10, 1975. It was a week during which the principal focus of interest was on southeast Asia: the insurgent forces in Cambodia were closing in on Phnom Penh, and the North Vietnamese and Vietcong had just launched what was to prove to be the last offensive of the Vietnam war. Dr. Kissinger was away in the Middle East, and I saw less of Mrs. Ford during the week than I had hoped, because she was in bed with an episode of the neck pain from which she had periodically suffered in recent years; otherwise, the week could probably have been described as a more or less typical one for the President.

In order to have an exact record of the President's

words, I taped two conversations with him, at breakfast on Thursday morning and after dinner on Friday evening in the residential part of the White House; I relied on my own notes to record all the other events of the week. The Press Office made no effort to steer me in any direction or to censor me in any way; a couple of members of the President's staff seemed rather more tempted to guide me or to gag me. Ron Nessen assigned an assistant, Larry Speakes, to me, with instructions, which Speakes ably carried out, to help me however I might ask to be helped, and to give me whatever documents I might want.

I was fearful that my mere presence might distort the discussions in the Oval Office, just as a known electronic bug might; but after the first day or so I felt I had been absorbed into the furniture. Sometimes the President would explain my presence to strangers; more often I think I was taken for a staffer whose job it apparently was to keep scribbling madly in an effort to record all Oval Office transactions, now that the infamous tapes were no longer being made.

The *Times*' gifted and tactful photographer, George Tames, popped unobtrusively in and out of meetings. This never caused any commotion, because photography was obviously an ever-present mania in the White House; for months on end the President's personal photographer, David Kennerly, or one of his staff had been clicking visual records of just about everything that had been going on.

Special thanks are due to DuPre Jones for invaluable help he gave me in research and checking, and to Robert Wool and David Anderson of the *Times* for support and vigilance in the close-in chores of getting the manuscript to press.

Members of the administration who figured in the events of the week are listed in an appendix, beginning on page 151, and they are identified with the posts they held at the time.

THE
PRESIDENT

MONDAY

A Stubborn Calm at the Center

Donald Rumsfeld, with a sheaf of papers under his arm, opens the staff door to the Oval Office and nods over his shoulder to me to follow him, and we walk in. The President, seated behind his desk, greets us; first names come easily to him, and because he and I have met before, he uses mine.

It is 8:33. Monday morning. A rainy day.

Rumsfeld pulls a chair up to a corner of the desk and puts the papers down. I sit against the curving east wall of the room, in a straight cane-backed chair. The President, holding a pipe to his mouth with his left hand, tips a butane lighter into it and puffs up a cloud.

The Assistant to the President begins talking and passing papers across the desk. A Navy steward in a red coat serves coffee. I am far too excited at first to be

3

able to follow what is being said. I am conscious of the arching energy, on a table just to my left, of Frederic Remington's sculpture "Bronco Buster," a cowboy bending to the rise of a violent caracole, the dark bronze horse under him seeming to explode with ferocity and joy. Not quite so sharply to my left is the utterly still figure beyond the desk, dark-suited, contained, reading some document his aide has handed him, pale drifting smoke the only motion there.

The President has given me permission to take a kind of voyage with him—to watch him closely through a working week. I have a unique opportunity, and at this moment its prospect staggers me. By the time the week is over, I will have been given access to a President of the United States of a sort no journalist has ever had. It is already clear that Mr. Ford is going to be even more open with me than was Harry Truman when, a quarter of a century ago, he allowed me a somewhat similar privilege. I will in fact be doing something that less than a handful of Mr. Ford's own staff of 533 has done: I will be with him, most of the time, hour in and hour out, through the whole week's range of his backbreaking routine.

I sit here trying to get my bearings. Charles Willson Peale's foxy and sexy old Ben Franklin is squinting disconcertingly at me from across the room through mod-looking spectacles. Over the mantel one of Peale's seven Washingtons, this portrait full-length, the face austere and disapproving, looks past me and straight at his distant successor, as if wondering, wondering. I am curious about the days ahead. I want to know what I suppose every citizen wants to know. Our country has been through agonies of failed leadership. Are we in the hands of steady men now? What is the quality of this quiet person murmuring to his aide? What is his style, and what secrets, if any, does it encode—or is all of him right out there on the surface? How does he make decisions? Is he bright enough? How stubborn is he? Is he at all flexible? Is the office changing him? Has he been able to lift his vision from the boundaries of the Fifth Congressional District of Michigan to the full sweep from Maine to Hawaii where the electorate lives that had no chance to choose him?

The figure behind the desk is drenched in the dazzling artificial light of this room. A dark pin-stripe suit, the lapels just the right width for this year; a tie slashed with bold diagonal stripes. I search the face, now tilting up from reading. There is a slight tuck on the lower right cheek, not matched on the left. Higher on the left cheek are three barely visible bumps, suddenly folded now into the creases of a smile. Which fades quickly. At the foot of the long slope of the bald forehead there are stark, slashing horizontal lines of the skinfold over the deepset sixty-one-year-old eyes that need no glasses for reading, and, beneath, two darkish puffy semicircles. The eyes seek Rumsfeld's. The strong impression I get is of total relaxation: The hand guides the pipe as if the pipe were free of gravity.

Rumsfeld is explaining something. His hands, held out before him on a plane parallel to the desk top, chop sharply thumb to thumb, then cut away from each other, the fingers fanning. Ford listens, puffs, says, "Let's get them in here and talk about it."

9:05 A.M. Jack Marsh is in the chair where Rumsfeld sat. "You saw the letter," the Counselor asks, "from thirty-seven Democrat freshmen opposing any further aid to Cambodia?"

"I read about it this morning."

The pipe is clamped in the right side of the mouth. The face gives no message. Strong eye contact is maintained.

"Here's a letter from fifteen Senators"—Marsh reaches it forward; says it proposes a candidate for Under Secretary of Transportation; summarizes the man's record; makes it clear that he has been a good political soldier.

"Give it to Bill Walker, Jack."

Beyond the Presidential desk from where I sit, a head of Harry Truman thrusts its feisty challenge into the room. The bronze face looks pleased, as if saying: Who'd have thought I'd be one of three past Presidents represented here?

The third is Abraham Lincoln, who stands, slender and brooding, on a pedestal on the east side of the room, to my right. Ford chose this company of three: Washington, Lincoln, Truman. Mrs. Ford found the Truman head abandoned in the White House warehouse.

9:18 A.M. Rumsfeld, Marsh, Hartmann, Nessen and Friedersdorf enter for the daily session preparing Ron Nessen for his briefing of the press. Ever since Watergate days, reporters' questions in these briefings have been searching, prolonged, often fierce—the sum of all the questions being: Does a President ever tell the truth?

As the men draw chairs around the desk, the President rises—what a big man he is!—steps to a table behind him, picks up four brand-new pipes, still in their store packages, and tosses one to each of the pipe smokers, Hartmann, Marsh, Rumsfeld and Nessen,

. . . with Marsh, Hartmann, Friedersdorf, Rumsfeld, Nessen

who has just switched from cigarettes. "Someone gave me these. I don't much care for that type of pipe," he says. Bright-colored pipes with meerschaum or plastic bowls and elaborate cooling stems. Marsh and Rumsfeld, knowing each other's color preferences, make a swap. The steward is passing coffee again. The President, who drank tea at breakfast, now takes his second cup of coffee.

NESSEN (*glasses parked on top of his head*): On Cambodia. I think I'll be getting flak from some things Humphrey said on "Face the Nation" yesterday—that aid wouldn't help the situation even if it got there. Hubert said he'd seen some C.I.A. cables that came to the same conclusion.

The Plexiglas-covered globe of the earth beyond the President's desk suddenly seems to jump up into full scale. Cambodia. I am all ears. The President, who has in recent days seemed to be completely out of touch with the mood of the country on the everlasting suffering of the Asian wars, is in a tight struggle with Congress—yet again—over emergency funds for both Vietnam and Cambodia. I can imagine Truman's explosion if he had been crossed on a conviction of his in this way by an old friend. No—Ford's tone, when he speaks, is exactly the tone he used when he was talking earlier about a prospective Under Secretary of Transportation: His utterance is slow; he pauses long at his mental commas; he almost never uhs; he speaks as if he means just these words and no other words would do.

FORD: What I've said was that if no aid was sent, it would be inevitable that the Government would fall; if it was sent, there'd be a fifty-fifty chance of survival till the rainy season, or roughly that.

RUMSFELD: In the senior staff meeting, Brent Scow-

9

croft said he knows what Humphrey saw, and it did not say that even if aid were sent the Government would fall. But I cautioned Ron about being too blunt here. There are bound to have been differing interpretations.

FORD: I agree. Point One (*he raises a straight right forefinger*), whatever Hubert saw, there could have been a phrase or a sentence that could have led him honestly to believe what he was saying, and Point Two (*his right hand comes up again, the forefinger and middle finger raised but bent; the hand is loose*), we don't know for sure everybody Hubert saw, or for that matter exactly what cables he saw.

HARTMANN: We do know that the public believes the President gets all the information and others only partial information. Don't call Hubert a liar. Say something like, "The President's best judgment is . . ."

MARSH: It's significant that he did tip his hat to you for supplying more information than in the past.

FORD (*leaning back in his shiny black leather swivel chair*): We made a conscious decision that Henry would go before Congress, or maybe a subcommittee, and give as much information as possible. That led Sparkman to come to his conclusion, which was to support the whole package, and it led Clifford Case to support substantially the whole package. Even in that group, though, who got a lot of facts, you have differences of opinion.

RUMSFELD: Ron, use Bob's point that we have all the information, and various people using the same information can come to different conclusions.

NESSEN: Then I'll say, based on the facts you have, Mr. President, you've concluded that there's a fifty-fifty chance of the Government's being able to carry on till the rainy season if aid is sent—

FORD (*holding up an arresting hand*): —in time. Ten days or two weeks.

NESSEN: What do I say to questions about their dickering for a lower figure?

FORD: In our discussions they suggest a lower figure. We believe our figure is right. They have the authority to set the figure. Henry made the point to the group that we want no part of giving too little. Better an adequate figure and an honest effort than too little.

MARSH: Wasn't it Churchill: "Too little and too late"?

HARTMANN: The Sudeten Plan. It was when Hitler . . .

9:50 A.M. The Nessen group departs.

Behind the President's big black seat at the desk, between it and the tall south windows, stands a wide table, on which, backed by two delicate silver Argand lamps designed for tubular wicks that once burned whale oil but now equipped with tiny, flame-shaped electric bulbs bravely glimmering in a sea of light, there are color photographs of Betty Ford; of all the Ford children at their father's swearing-in, with Jack in the foreground; of Mike and his wife, Gayle; of Steve and his bright jeep; of Susan and her cat, Shan; and of the family's golden retriever, Liberty, on the White House lawn. Papers that the President must read, most of them in separate blue folders, are stacked in front of these pictures on the table, and Mr. Ford swivels now to pick up the pile and lift it to his desk.

He takes a fresh pipe from the top right-hand drawer of his desk, packs it and lights it. The steward comes in to remove cups and rearrange chairs. The President reads a personal communication from Secretary of State Kissinger, who is away, shuttling; and a long briefing paper for a meeting the President is to have be-

fore lunch with Dr. Arthur Burns, Chairman of the Federal Reserve Board.

After a time, Mr. Ford rings for Terry O'Donnell, the keeper of the staff door, and asks him to have some photographs delivered to Mrs. Ford, for her to autograph for friends. Later O'Donnell comes in with some commissions to sign, among them the certificates of appointment of Carla Hills, the new Secretary of Housing and Urban Development, who is to be sworn in at noon on this day, and of John Dunlop, the new Secretary of Labor, who is to be installed next week.

The President begins reading again.

I feel that, no matter how still I sit, I am a distraction, and I leave the Oval Office.

·   ·   ·

I listen to Ron Nessen's briefing on a monitor in his office. It turns out that after all the time spent with the President on Hubert Humphrey and Cambodia, there is not a single question from reporters on the war. Instead there is a ferocious grilling that starts with a question whether the President had been informed at any time by William E. Colby, Director of the Central Intelligence Agency, or by any other C.I.A. official, "that the late Senator Robert Kennedy had told two associates that he had vetoed or been able to veto a plan —this question takes a long time to ask because it is a complicated thing—the C.I.A. plan to contract with the Mafia to assassinate Prime Minister Castro."

NESSEN (*after a pause for thought*): I am not going to say anything about that, Jim.

Q: Will we ever find out anything about that, or the previous story about the C.I.A. assassination allegations which were asked about last week; that is, is the White House ever going to have anything to say about those stories?

NESSEN: Right now, I am not going to say anything about it, Walt.

Q: Last week you said a number of things. Why are you not going to say anything about it?

NESSEN: I can't.

All during the press conference, reporters keep coming back and back to this subject, and fourteen more times Nessen says, in one phrasing or another, "I am just not going to talk about that."

11:51 A.M. During the meeting with the Nessen group, the President asked to see "the latest go-round on the Carla Hills thing," and now Bob Hartmann, who is in charge of speechwriters, and Bob Orben, one of them,

. . . with Orben and Hartmann

bring in the final draft of the President's remarks for the swearing-in.

It suddenly seems that Cambodia and the C.I.A. might as well be on the moon.

"I thought I might have a little fun with Carla to disavow my male chauvinism," the President says.

"You have to be careful there, Mr. President," Orben says. "That's suddenly a *verboten* area. In no part of the speech do we refer to her as a woman."

"Betty's been out in front on this Equal Rights Amendment business, and I'd like to get something in. Can't we do something with the budget side of it? You know, like a household budget. Let's see." He looks at the text. "The budget gives her a lot more than was given to Jim Lynn"—her male predecessor, still in the Cabinet as Director of the Office of Management and

Budget. "That doesn't sound like male chauvinism to me. Why don't you fool around with that?"

12:07 P.M. He stands at a lectern on a podium in the East Room of the residence, alongside Secretary-Designate Hills and flanked by her husband, her children dressed to the nines, the Vice President and a ceremonial delegation of Senators and Congressmen. The room is murmurous with standing guests. Television lights are on. The President places his speech on the lectern, and a respectful silence falls.

"I am in very good company," he starts out, "welcoming Carla into the Cabinet as Secretary of Housing and Urban Development. Carla; Mr. Justice White, who is about to administer the oath; HUD Under Secretary

. . . with Senators Cranston and Brooke, Hills, Rockefeller, and the Hills children

Jim Mitchell; and I are all graduates of Yale Law
School.

"Maybe I better not say that too loudly. I can imagine a dozen other prospects starting to practice the
'Whiffenpoof Song.' (*Half-hearted laughter*) . . ."

This voice is different from the relaxed one I have
been hearing all morning. Of course, it is amplified;
perhaps the amplifier has wooden parts. I have heard
that Gerald Ford loves to make speeches. That he loves
to sit for hours at luncheons eating bad food and listening to worse speeches than his own. That for years he
has been flying here and there across the country
carrying the Republican word. Recently he hired a
former producer for CBS News, Robert Mead, to give
him pointers, and Mead has been trying to help the
President loosen up. He has urged speechwriters to provide texts early, so the President could read them out
loud several times to get his mouth comfortably around
the written words. "It's hard to vocal some of those long
sentences," Mr. Mead says. He has been trying to
stamp out some of Mr. Ford's Grand Rapids pronunci-
ations: "guahrantee," "judgament." But Gerald Ford
has very likely uttered five million words in speeches
on and off the floor of the House, and as Vice President
and President, and he is, I am beginning to see, a man
of intransigent habits. Right now, introducing Carla
Hills, he is his old speaking self. Besides, his arms and
hands, which all morning have been gliding as grace-
fully as the smoke that played games around them,
have gone rubbery—though it must at least be said that
his gestures, unlike Mr. Nixon's, have a direct connec-
tion with what he is saying. I get a lift from his awk-
wardness. I am glad that President Ford is a hard case
for the hired image-makers. Here his stubbornness will

help us all. It is likely that the real Gerald Ford, for better or for worse, will always be visible and audible to the citizenry, no matter how hard the experts try to disguise him.

Now he praises Mrs. Hills, refers to the Housing and Community Development Act of 1974, and says, "One of Carla's major jobs will be to implement this massive and, I believe, progressive program. Incidentally, Carla's budget for fiscal 1976 will be $7.1 billion. That is $1.6 billion more than was given to her predecessor, Jim Lynn. Now if that does not dispose of male chauvinism, nothing will." (*A pretty good laugh.*)

12:19 P.M. The President walks from the East Room along the brilliant red carpet of the cross hall, past the flags, past the aggressive Houdon bust of Joel Barlow, under the twinkling Adam chandeliers, past the proud Hoban columns like marble guardsmen—beyond whose picket line crimson-coated musicians of the United States Marine Band, their violins soaring to salute the chief, play from the score of a moving picture called *Villa Rides*—past black ushers, past uniformed aides, past Secret Service operatives with radio wires dribbling down from their right ears under their jacket collars, past notables and bureaucrats and toadies, breasting all the pomp with his brisk stride, which is loose-haunched and shoulder-floating, like that of a fettlesome quarterhorse.

In the State Dining Room he receives guests beside his new HUD Secretary, and he chats without haste with those who push their faces close to his.

12:36 P.M. He is back in the Oval Office, at his desk, his chin resting on his left hand. Dr. Arthur Burns, Chairman of the Federal Reserve Board, whose gray hair seems not to be receding but actually to be advancing down his forehead, leans over the end of the desk to the President's right, shuffling papers. David Kennerly, the President's personal photographer, who is bearded and brassy, and who well knows that the most abashing eye on earth to men of power is the camera's winking lens, comes in to snap some shots. Kennerly, or one of his four assistants, makes a record of every appointment the President has, except for those with his closest staff. Perhaps these are "for history" in lieu of the Nixon tapes. Mr. Ford pleases many of his visitors by seeing that they receive photographs, later, of themselves in easy intimacy with the President of the United States.

The President has a number of questions he wants to ask: How soon will there be signs of economic recovery, and how strong will it be? Is the money supply going to continue to rise? Fast enough to promote recovery? Not so fast as to reignite inflation? Inflation is slowing down—is this a permanent reduction or is there still an underlying problem of inflation that will reappear when the economy begins to turn around? What will be the effects of larger-than-budgeted Federal deficits?

Dr. Burns, in a quiet, rather high-pitched voice, gives the President a thorough explanation of monetary and economic trends; the meeting, scheduled for thirty minutes, lasts sixty-five. Dr. Burns has brought several charts; on some of them upwardness is visible.

1:41 P.M. Enter, breathlessly, Miss Shirley Cothran, of Denton, Texas, Miss America of 1975, who has had to cool her nifty heels for forty minutes while the President and Dr. Burns were having their *tête-à-tête*. Miss America is accompanied by Doris Kelly, a young lady who is described as her chaperone; by her Congressman, Ray Roberts; and by Mayor Joseph A. Bradway of Atlantic City, where she was crowned.

The President, apparently bucked up by what he has heard about money, now seems to have no difficulty whatsoever wrenching his attention away from the economy.

FORD: Nice to meet you, Shirley.

MISS AMERICA (*memorization straining every sweet muscle of her face*): I have presents here, sir, for you, and also one for Mrs. Ford.

FORD: My wife and I watch the Miss America contest all the time. We really enjoy that on TV.

MISS AMERICA: I sure hope you saw it this year. That was the best year.

FORD: It sure was!

ROBERTS: My most famous constituent, Mr. President, and, I may say, my most beautiful one.

FORD: I thought all the girls down there in Texas looked like this, Ray.

Now comes a stampede of pool photographers with still and motion-picture and TV cameras, and with hooded lights on long wires. The President and his little party are herded toward the east side of the room. David Kennerly, who has grown familiar with his boss, says, "Would you mind putting her in the middle, please?" "Not 'her,' David," the President says. "Her name is Shirley. Where are your manners?"

Miss America runs off to the side to put down her purse, which may not look nice in the photos. While cameras click, the President, taking advantage of a briefing, which has informed him that Shirley has

studied at North Texas State University and plans to be an elementary-school guidance counselor, is chatting with her in a low voice. "How long will that take? ... That's wonderful. ... Fine new buildings you have there. ..."

"Thirty seconds, please," Assistant Press Secretary Bill Roberts calls out to the photographers. Then: "Lights, please. Thank you." And out goes the pool.

MISS AMERICA (*in haste, sensing that she herself is being eased toward the door*): As I travel around, people ask me about all kinds of things, Mr. President, and I'm only twenty-two years old, but I really can say that I support you in every single thing you do.

FORD: I really appreciate that, Shirley. Going back to school next fall?

MISS AMERICA: In January.

FORD: I'm certain that after a hard year it will be welcome.

MISS AMERICA: Sure hope you have a chance to visit North Texas State again, sir.

FORD: Real nice to see you, Shirley. Congratulations and good luck.

Miss America looks flustered and puzzled. The President realizes why, before anyone else in the room does, possibly even before Miss America herself. "Hey," he says. "Better not leave your purse, Shirley. We've got some real bad characters around here."

1:45 P.M. The President has fifteen minutes for lunch before the next scheduled appointment. He ducks into a small private room off the Oval Office that Betty Ford has been fixing up for him as a kind of hideaway.

I retire to the staff anteroom. So far I have had a sense of rushing after the President from one isolated fragment of administration or ceremony or politics or planning to another and another. I realize that I am still slightly agog, and that I have suddenly cut across the grain into a continuous timber of the Presidential process. But I wonder: When is policy made? When is thinking done? How have I missed scenes of the tense struggle over Cambodian funds? I have seen so many new faces; perhaps in time I can sort them out. I feel hurried. But here in the anteroom Terry O'Donnell, the young man who juggles people and papers in and out of the Oval Office, and Nell Yates, who keeps the logs and assists O'Donnell, are calm. Come to think of it, everyone I have seen today has been calm. And the center of the calm, its essence and source, has obviously been the President. With Truman it was all nervous energy, moral intensity, emotion in harness, history clamoring for expression. Here the strongest impression, so far, is of relaxation.

1:55 P.M. The President, it turns out, has taken only ten minutes to eat. He calls me in and tells me that it will not be appropriate for me to sit in on the next meeting, which is to be in the Cabinet Room. "This isn't really my party," he says. "The Chief Justice asked if he could come in to see me, and we've got the leaders of Congress, too. This is a historic get-together. I don't know as there's ever been a summit meeting of all three branches of Government in the White House like this in recent times—certainly not in my memory since I became Minority Leader." He motions me to a seat. "Let me tell you about the meeting."

I am impressed in these few minutes by the President's courtesy and trust; with one or two exceptions, members of his staff have been far more cautious or manipulative than he in dealing with me. He really does seem to be an open man. I am touched that he rushed his already meager lunch period in order to give me this time. I take note, too, as he talks, of his grasp of the briefing he has had.

"We have a tough decision," he says. "There hasn't been increased compensation for the Judiciary since '69 and there has been a 44.5-percent increase in the cost of living since then. This is particularly serious in the court system, because most real fine lawyers get more than the $40,000 District judges get, or the $42,000 that Appeals Court judges get, or even the $60,000 that Supreme Court Justices get, or the $62,500 the Chief Justice gets. The Chief Justice thinks the courts aren't getting, or else they're losing, their best judges on account of this. We have the same problem in the Executive Branch, where the ceiling is $36,000. We're losing top people both in the military and the State Department. Congress is having similar problems. The Chief Justice strongly feels that Congress ought to separate out the Judiciary from Congress and the Executive, but I doubt if this will be possible. The political environment is not right for increases. Congress isn't in the mood for them. I myself have suggested a 5-percent one-year cap on all Government increases. Under the present system the cost-of-living increase would amount to something like 9 percent. If you coordinate that with 5-percent increases in all three branches, the first-year cost would be $1,159,400 for the Congress, $1,039,250 for the Judiciary, $1,496,725 for the Executive, and—I was astonished at this—$27,450,000 for the military. An arrangement like this wouldn't catch the Judiciary up, but it would give some relief and then keep them current. I don't know. We're going to have to work something out to keep our best people in Government."

2:01 P.M. He takes me into the Cabinet Room for the opening moments of the meeting, when the pool cameramen will in any case be present.

Chief Justice Warren Burger, Speaker of the House Carl Albert, Senate Majority Leader Mike Mansfield, Senate Minority Leader Hugh Scott, House Minority Leader John Rhodes are waiting for Mr. Ford. The warmth of the greetings is abounding. Cambodia, energy, taxes—all quarrels are forgotten. Here enemies seem to be in love.

FORD: All three branches—

A Senator: A three-ring circus.
Burger (*seeing the other two branches in such intimate embraces*): I feel as if I ought to be on the other side of the table.
Ford: In judgament?
Burger: In the dock!

Re-entering the Oval Office alone, I feel its great force.

This room is an egg of light. I have seen that each person who comes into it is lit up in two senses: bathed in brightness and a bit high. I have clearly seen each face, to the very pores, in a flood of indirect candlepower that rains down from a pure-white ceiling onto the curving off-white walls and a pale-yellow rug and bright furnishings in shades of gold, green and salmon. But there are also dazzling parabolas of power here; authority seems to be diffused as an aspect of the artificial light in the room, and each person who comes into this heady glow seems to be rendered ever so slightly tipsy in it and by it—people familiar with the room far less so, of course, than first-time visitors, some of whom visibly goggle and stagger and hold on tight as they make their appeals; but even the old hands, even the President's closest friends, and even the President himself, sitting in a bundle of light behind the desk of the chief, seem to me to take on a barely perceptible extra shine in the ambiguous radiant energy that fills this room.

Gerald Ford wanted, and was entitled to, an Oval Office in his own style. His wife helped him achieve it. Only a few traces remain of the Nixon Oval Office, with its ostentatious expense-account taste: the Peale Washington; a picture by an unknown artist of the mid-nineteenth century, called "The President's House"; the vulgar gold curtains behind the President's desk; the desk itself; and a few chairs. The vile bugs that fed the tapes are gone; when President Ford learned that a device, though dead, was still embedded in the desk, he had it rooted out. Mrs. Ford, assisted by the tasteful Curator of the White House, Clement E. Conger, planned a thoroughgoing redecoration, and during the President's trip to Vladivostok the transformation was made.

Some exquisite pieces were brought into the room— a Massachusetts Hepplewhite-style chest of drawers, for instance, on which the Truman head stands, with a serpentine front and fan inlay quadrants on the drawers; and a Federal card table made in Salem, Massachusetts, about 1810, whose top is supported by a large, carved, gilded, spread-winged eagle—the only known table of its kind in America. Most beautiful of all, to my mind, is a grandfather clock, designed by John and Thomas Seymour of Boston in the early nineteenth century, with fluted columns at the corners and beautiful satinwood inlays; its forceful ticking inexorably marks the moments of history—and of nonhistory—in this room of light.

And so the room now is elegant, but the President's own territory, on and around his desk, is simple, and is comfortable for him. Centered on the desk in front of him is a metal football, raised from a penholder base, with a plate inscribed SOUTH HIGH FOOTBALL CLUB. It is from the teammates with whom he still has occasional reunions. To his right, next to the desk, is a side table with shelves for smoking things. Next to that, on the floor, is the brown suitcase in which he carries papers back and forth to the residence each evening and on weekends. His whole family is on the table close behind him.

3:19 P.M. The President is back. Secretary of Health, Education and Welfare Caspar Weinberger and Rumsfeld enter.

The President and the Secretary have been to the same party last night.

WEINBERGER: Thanks for last night. That was fun.

FORD: Barbra Streisand's a real good entertainer.

WEINBERGER: She is. I'd never known much about James Caan. . . .

The President, leaning back at ease in his big chair, and placing his hands together, fingertip to fingertip, praises the job that Cap, as he calls the Secretary, has been doing in H.E.W., and asks him to stay on in the Cabinet.

FORD: Every President has to have his own Cabinet and his imprint on a Cabinet, but I never agreed with those demands for wholesale resignations in 1973.

WEINBERGER: That first Cabinet meeting after the '72 election was the most shocking thing I've ever been through. Such a contrast to your first meeting, Mr. President. There wasn't a person who'd been at that earlier meeting who wasn't impressed with the difference.

Secretary Weinberger thanks the President for the great honor of his invitation to stay. He says he is fifty-seven years old, and for seven years he has been away from "an income-production situation." His wife, he says, has had a great deal of discomfort from osteo-arthritis and is anxious to get back to California. . . .

"I didn't know Jane was that adversely affected," the President says. "I'm sorry, Cap. Betty has something like that, I guess you know. She's been having some trouble ɛgain this week. She has this pinched nerve, you knovʾ—gives her a whole lot of discomfort. She has a great deal of fortitude, though. She bounces back."

After some further exchanges the Secretary again thanks the President for the great compliment, and says he will give an answer very soon.

3:48 P.M. The President receives Bob Hartmann and three speechwriters, Theis, Friedman and Orben. Two speeches are in the works. One is to be a light affair at a dinner of the Radio and Television Correspondents Association. "It's a fun occasion," Orben says. "Nothing serious. They're going to have Charlie Byrd, a jazz musician, then Bob Hope for fifteen or twenty minutes; then you'll follow."

FORD (*with a laugh that is not altogether comfortable*): Why do I always have to be hooked up with Hope and these pros? (*Starts reading a preliminary draft. He again laughs: this is his infectious boomer. Then, after a pause*): What's this about Judge Crater? Who's Judge Crater?

ORBEN: That's a milking laugh after the big one—

HARTMANN: Judge Crater was a prominent judge of the thirties who disappeared, and—

FORD: Why don't we leave that one out? . . .

A serious speech is scheduled for Notre Dame next week, and the President reads several pages of a draft. Then he breaks off.

FORD: The only problem I have with this—and maybe I misinterpret the attitudes of college students today—but I think they're moving away from the views of the last five years. I'm concerned about building rather than tearing apart. We don't want to repeat the mistakes of the sixties—or of the thirties. We want them to prepare themselves to avoid those mistakes. We need a subject that's meaningful—I'd think a foreign-policy topic. Not condemning the generation that ran things the last ten years, but looking back to the mistakes of the thirties and fifties.

THEIS: Father Hesburgh, who was a leader of the anti-war movement, strongly suggested we avoid Southeast Asia. The subject of hunger—

FORD: I'm not talking about Vietnam or Cambodia. I'm talking about a positive approach—that this generation of college students shouldn't fall into the trap of the college students of the thirties, of being oblivious to Europe's problems and those of the rest of the world.

HARTMANN: The timing's bad. Cambodia is going to be coming to a head, and anything you say is going to be read by the press as another plea for aid.

The President has put his feet up on his pipestand side table. Suggestions from the speechwriters begin to swirl around him, but even I can see that an idea had lodged itself in his mind, and is there to stay.

"Higher education in the private sector . . ." "Office of liaison in the White House for higher education . . ." "College presidents . . ." "A quasi-governmental agency, where kids can buy tuition bonds . . ." "Going without dinners, eating rice in the dining halls . . ." "Notre Dame prides itself on bringing students from abroad . . ." "Peace between generations . . ."

The Presidential feet come down.

FORD: O.K. Let's think about the theme of staying involved in the world. You know, Kennedy made the Peace Corps proposal at Ann Arbor. I think the Peace Corps, with all its critics, has been a good program. The U.S. has had a great record of being humanitarian. The first foreign policy I voted for in Congress in 1945 was on the Marshall Plan—that was a great humanitarian one. If you go back to the post–World-War-II period— the Marshall Plan was nonmilitary. The best commencement speech I ever gave was at Mike's commencement at Wake Forest. I didn't want to lecture them but wanted them to be better than we had been. Disciplined freedom—here (*reaching for his brown suitcase*), I have it right here. *My* files are the only ones I trust. Here. (*He reads:*) "Of course, the young generation knows perfectly well that we senior citizens were never your age, that we were born on the threshold of senility, and that whatever we think we remember about our youth is inaccurate and irrelevant. . . ."

4:40 P.M. Rumsfeld, Marsh and Counsel Buchen talk with the President on sensitive matters of personnel. I am not present.

6:05 P.M. I sit by while Rumsfeld goes over a wide range of matters, many of which are ready for the President's initials. Mr. Ford writes with his left hand, the hand curving above the writing. My thrilled agitation of the morning has given way to dazed exhaustion. I am still profoundly disturbed by what seemed to me the aimlessness of the speechwriting session—though I realize there will be another round on the Notre Dame speech, perhaps several more rounds. I keep thinking, however, of a speechwriting session of Harry Truman's, at which most of his principal advisers, including Dean Acheson, were present, and during which policy was really and carefully shaped through its

articulation. But now Rumsfeld, with his endless vo-
cabulary of hand signals—stabbings, long-fingered
rounding out of abstractions, flat-handed layering of
relationships, squarings off, chops, slaps, flicks,
pinches, punches, piano playing and a bit of harp work
—gives concise and brisk explanations of items he
raises, and President Ford, in no hurry, makes decisions as they are needed.

7:20 P.M. After eleven hours and forty-four minutes of
work in the West Wing (this does not, of course, include reading done in the residence between 5:30 and
7:30 in the morning, nor reading to be done there later
this evening), the President goes "home."

TUESDAY

A Hard-edged Conservative Voice

7:40 A.M. The President, accompanied by two Secret Service men and a valet carrying the brown suitcase, arrives from the residence. He is dressed today in a flashy suit of bold vertical stripes of shades of gray; he looks a bit drawn this morning. It is raining again.

7:42 A.M. Brent Scowcroft goes in to show the President dispatches from Henry Kissinger and intelligence messages that have accumulated overnight. I am not invited to join them; the President, in setting the ground rules for my access to him, has specifically excluded these daily foreign-policy and security sessions.

Lieutenant General Scowcroft, who is fifty, is Deputy Assistant to the President for National Security Affairs.

This means—though you would never know it to look at him—that he is Henry Kissinger's administrative *alter ego;* when the Secretary of State is away, and he is often away, the general alone speaks for him to the President on foreign and national-security matters. Short, wiry, rooster-quick, with sparkling eyes, he seems a living model of a sprite that must surely dwell in Dr. Henry Kissinger, who cannot possibly be as heavy and lugubrious all the way through as he looks and sounds on the outside. As to point of view, Scowcroft does in some eerie way actually seem to inhabit Kissinger. The general is a rarity—an intellectual soldier. He has a Ph.D. from Columbia in international relations; he has studied at West Point, Lafayette, Georgetown, the Strategic Intelligence School, the Armed Forces Staff College and the National War College; and he has been an assistant professor of Russian history at West Point and professor of political science at the Air Force Academy.

8:30 A.M. Robert Trowbridge Hartmann, with whom I now enter the Oval Office, is one of the President's two Counselors; he is fifty-eight. His explicit areas of responsibility are speechwriting and, vaguely, politics, but he is a long-standing friend of Mr. Ford's and was his Chief of Staff during the Vice Presidency, and he talks about all sorts of things with him now. Hearty, bluff, gray-haired, ruddy, he was once Washington bureau chief for *The Los Angeles Times,* and he is shrewd and accurate in assessing how the press will respond to whatever the President does. He has a mischievous look in his eye as he hands the President a strip of teletype, saying, "You'll be happy to see that Martha Mitchell is against you."

The President reads and laughs. "That's a cheery note at eight in the morning," he says.

Hartmann hands him another item—some not-so-cheery news about conservative Republicans; and an announcement that the Senate is planning to recess for Easter in just ten days—which allows a very short time for the struggles over taxes and Cambodian aid.

He tells the President that a delegation from the Gridiron Club—"the Privy Council of the Press"—seeks an audience with him to present a formal invitation to this year's dinner.

He gives the President a speech Ford had made at William and Mary, as possible background for an interview he is to have later in the day with the editors of *Fortune,* on the development of American institutions.

Then Hartmann says that Jack Stiles, a Grand Rapids newspaperman who collaborated with Ford on *Portrait of the Assassin,* a book that was a by-product of Ford's service on the Warren Commission, wants some information from the President's personal files.

Now I have a moment of seeing the President as an author, with the look on his face of one who may have a deal in the works.

THE AUTHOR: M-G-M contacted me about taking *Portrait* and making a documentary of it. Buchen turned them down. Then M-G-M contacted Jack, and he went to California for a day or so. They want to make three two-hour documentaries, using *Portrait* as a theme. Our book took the testimony of witnesses from the report, and it backed up the commission's finding that Oswald did it alone. Simon and Schuster's thinking of republishing it. Jack wants to find out how the radio and television rights stand. With all these charges of assassination plots against Castro and everything, there may be some interest. I still think the way we used the witnesses' testimony was: Number One (*the forefinger rises to the count*), more readable than the report and than the other books that were critical . . .

The President does not get beyond Number One.

8:35 A.M. The senior staff meeting is apparently lasting somewhat longer than usual this morning, and Rumsfeld's deputy, Richard Cheney, fills in for him while he is delayed.

Right away, Cheney brings up a sticky item. In his first State-of-the-Union Message, in January, urging "energy independence," the President asked Congress to authorize full-scale commercial development of the naval petroleum reserve at Elk Hills, California. Out of the blue, a few days later, without having notified the Administration, the Standard Oil Company of California announced its intention of pulling its drilling rigs out of Elk Hills in order to avoid possible criticism of its role there. (Elk Hills was one of the reserves involved in the Teapot Dome scandal of 1923.) The Navy, Cheney says, has not yet found a new operator and he raises the question whether the reserve should be transferred from Navy to Interior Department control.

FORD: I'm more interested in getting action, getting production, getting oil, than I am in what agency runs the place. On my next trip West I want to go out there and see first-hand what Elk Hills looks like. I'm disturbed nothing's happening there. I'd like to get some action. We're interested in substance, not jurisdiction!

8:50 A.M. Donald Rumsfeld, who comes in now, is by far the most equal of the theoretically equal top members of Mr. Ford's staff. He is also, at forty-two, the youngest of them. His gift is for organization. He is the only member of the staff frequenting the Oval Office in whose eye I think I can see, now and then, behind his fashionable "aviator" glasses with their delicate black rims, a glint that seems to say, "That big leather chair on the other side of the desk looks comfortable. I wonder if it would fit me." He is bright, jealous, crafty and fiercely combative; he once captained the Princeton wrestling team. He served four terms in Congress, representing the wealthy North Shore above Chicago, and his voting record was almost identical with Gerald Ford's. He is a Nixon holdover—campaigned for him in '66, ran the Office of Economic Opportunity for him awhile, and in 1970 entered the White House as his Counselor and Director of his Cost of Living Council. To Rumsfeld's credit, he eventually was given the shudders by Haldeman and Ehrlichman, and he had himself shot out as far away from them as he could be—to Brussels, as Ambassador to NATO. President Ford called him home from there. His active hands move as if blown by every gust in his mind—always shaping, shaping, grasping bits of form out of the chaos of power.

Now, taking over from Cheney, he reviews the senior staff meeting and helps the President plan the rest of the day.

9:07 A.M. As Jack Marsh is about to enter the Oval Office, someone hands him an urgent cable for the President's eyes. Marsh reads it. He says to Terry O'Donnell, "Get General Scowcroft. The President's going to want to ask him some questions about this." He enters and hands the paper to the President. It is from

Ambassador Frank Carlucci in Lisbon, and it informs the President of an uprising against the Portuguese Government by air-force units. Scowcroft is soon at attention before the big desk.

FORD (*unflapped*): Do we have any information that their air force has been unhappy?

SCOWCROFT: Not particularly, as a whole. Two or three weeks ago there were some rumors of a possible coup, primarily, it was thought, in armed forces guarding—

FORD: Any philosophical differences between the airforce group and other army units?

SCOWCROFT: Not that we know of. As a practical matter, it would be difficult for the air force to mount a coup.

FORD: Keep me posted, Brent.

SCOWCROFT: I will, Mr. President.

FORD: I'm glad we've got Frank Carlucci over there. He's a good man. Any further word from Henry?

SCOWCROFT: Yes, sir. I'll bring it in later. From Turkey. Not particularly encouraging. (*He leaves.*)

John O. Marsh, Jr., who is forty-eight, and who, as Counselor, is in over-all charge of the President's relations with Congress and with various sectors of the public, including businessmen, women, minorities and consumers, has a way of pointing at a photograph over the mantel in his office of his farm in the Virginia hills and, with a slanting look just above and off to one side of his interlocutor's forehead, saying, "That's my little shanty in Strasburg. I'm just a country lawyer." Roughly translated, this means: "Watch out, my friend —take a good grip on your credit cards." Jack Marsh was in Congress with Gerald Ford—as a Byrd Democrat. Now calling himself an independent, he is ideologically much the most conservative man in the inner circle on the staff (in the 90th Congress, Gerald Ford voted 63 percent of the time with the so-called conservative coalition of Republicans and Southern Democrats; Marsh voted with the coalition 98 percent of the time), yet he seems personally the most sensitive and humane man in the group.

MARSH: Did you see that they've got this $6-billion bill up there to create jobs? They apparently put it together quietly in committee. . . .

By now I have noticed that whereas the Nixon insiders used the word "they" when speaking of hostile forces, the press, demonstrators, enemies, all who were considered threatening, this Administration uses it exclusively for a single, solid and frustrating entity—the Democratic majority in Congress.

FORD: Let's get some more information on the bill. . . .

MARSH: I've been talking with some folks from Chrysler, and they feel there's maybe too much bad news about the economy coming out of here. They were talking about boat shows. They've been doing real well, selling lots and lots of big craft. Sales are down on the blue-collar lines, the small boats, but they're real happy over-all. Chrysler boat sales are up and auto sales are down. Maybe we ought to take hold of some signs. . . .

Now Marsh brings up a sensitive matter. *The Washington Star-News* has carried a story that Representative John Rhodes, the man who succeeded Gerald Ford as Minority Leader of the House and an old friend of his, has announced that House Republicans are going to develop a legislative program of their own, separate from the President's. He has been quoted to the effect that "the days Republicans can get elected on somebody else's coattails are gone, gone forever."

MARSH: I'm not that upset about it, Mr. President. . . .

The President's face is a mask. I can see no surprise, no hurt, no anger.

9:20 A.M. The Nessen group comes in.

NESSEN: I had a big go-round on the C.I.A. in yesterday's briefing. I'd like to ask you this: What are your personal views on the use of assassination?

Here I do see a moment's flash of the Truman style. Mr. Ford's answer is an immediate reflex.

FORD (*leaning forward, striking the edge of the desk repeatedly with a forefinger*): I've been assured it's not going on, and I don't want it to go on.

Nessen gives a full account of the ferocity of the questioning in yesterday's briefing. The range of allegations, he says, is widening, to the point of speculation that the C.I.A. may have been involved in one of the Kennedy assassinations, or both. What is he to say about all these things?

A long discussion ensues, about who is, or should be, checking out allegations of past plots by the C.I.A. The question is not settled here; it will be taken forward.

And I have seen one way in which policy is spurred, if not engendered.

The Rhodes embarrassment is discussed. Rumsfeld bitterly says he thinks the Republicans on the Hill have been watching the President slide in the polls and "are trying to put some light between them and you. Wait till the polls go up again: then they'll come running."

FORD: John's all right. I don't worry about him.

HARTMANN: It's like when I was writing papers for the Republican Policy Committee—remember, Mr. President?—and we called them Constructive Republican

Alternative Proposals. It didn't take those clever Democrat lads long to find out what the initials spelled.

Hearing this, I suddenly remember the parentheses marking deleted expletives marching like an army of ants across the Nixon transcripts, and I realize that I have yet to hear—except in Hartmann's acronym, to cheer the President up—a single four-letter word in this room.

Max L. Friedersdorf, Assistant to the President for Legislative Affairs, gives a report on how the President's request for $222 million in emergency aid for Cambodia stands in a Senate Foreign Relations subcommittee and in a House Foreign Affairs subcommittee, and how the dickering on the tax-cut bill is coming along in the House Ways and Means Committee. Friedersdorf, a tall blond Hoosier, a former newspaperman, is in complete command of his material; he has preliminary counts on how the votes will go in various committees. The President, thoroughly at home with Congressional give-and-take, talks zestfully, predicting how this man and that man will finally come down. He names some who are dead set against him; he speaks their first names with fondness.

The prospects are bleak. It is hard to understand why the President, who has made so much of the need for this aid, is not upset.

10:50 A.M. The President receives a young lady who has been designated Maid of Cotton for 1975. This stunt is a replica of yesterday's reception of Miss America, except that it has more crassly commercial overtones.

.   .   .

. . . with the Maid of Cotton

At his press briefing a few minutes later, Ron Nessen tells the mediamen about the visit to the Oval Room of the Maid of Cotton, who in real life is Miss Kathryn Tenkhoff, of Sikeston, Missouri.

NESSEN: Secretary Butz also attended the meeting.

Q: Did Butz come over just for that?

NESSEN: Cotton is his area of responsibility.

Q: How much cotton do they grow in Missouri?

NESSEN: They grow cotton queens in Missouri. They grow cotton somewhere else.

11:01 A.M. The first sharp shock of the week is in store for me.

Assembled in the Cabinet Room are all the Administration's big guns on the economy and energy: the President himself; Vice President Nelson Rockefeller; Secretary of the Treasury William Simon; the President's Cabinet-rank Assistant for Economic Affairs, William Seidman; the new Secretary of Labor, John Dunlop; James Lynn of the Office of Management and Budget; Chairman Alan Greenspan of the Council of Economic Advisers; Chairman Frank Zarb of the Energy Resources Council; Dr. Burns of the Fed; Rumsfeld, Hartmann, Scowcroft and some staff assistants.

The President asks Secretary Simon for a report on the status of the tax-rebate bill.

SIMON: Mr. President, we're attempting to keep this to a temporary, one-shot thing. As you know, the House has proposed a $21.3-billion rebate using more or less our method, but lowering the income allowance. No one in his right mind believes that when they get going on this it'll be temporary. On the Senate bill, I went up and testified before the Senate Finance Committee, and I guess a ball-park figure of where they'll come out would be $25 billion, and you can bet your hat the House won't be able to resist matching those goodies. . . .

FORD: Any chance of lifting the $200 ceiling on individual rebates?

SIMON: There's a fair shot of getting $500. Mr. President, this whole deal of theirs is more of a welfare thing than anything else. They're making the assumption that low-income people should get more than their share of the giveaway. It's just a welfare thing, Mr. President.

FORD: Let me ask you this: I have two sons who worked last summer and earned about $1,500 each. Would they get $100 rebate?

SIMON: In my judgment, absolutely.

FORD: That's ridiculous.

SIMON: If they're typical of young people who work in the summertime—

FORD: It's ridiculous.

SIMON: I couldn't agree more, Mr. President.

SEIDMAN: Essentially it gives them back their Social Security tax.

SIMON: That's exactly what it does.

HARTMANN: But if they go out and spend it—

FORD: They'll spend it, all right! (*Laughter.*)

A little later:

FORD: What's going on about the oil-depletion allowance?

SIMON: I think they're cutting a deal up there right now. . . .

FORD (*after more discussion*): Our position should be that we do not want a Christmas-tree bill, with a whole lot of favors and gifts attached to it, and we've got to attack the whole issue of including cutting out the oil-depletion allowance in the tax-stimulus bill.

This was the first time I had seen the President and the Vice President in the same room. They now face each other on opposite sides of the center of the long Cabinet table. The President, as usual, is still, controlled, imperturbable. The Vice President, by contrast, is as active as a two-month-old kitten. He slumps, shoots bolt upright, leans to one side, then to the other, whispers, nods when he agrees, shakes his head when he differs. Now he speaks up.

ROCKEFELLER: Is it too late to propose an excess-profits

42

tax on the oil companies with an allowance for plow-back?

SIMON: It is, sir. We've proposed a windfall-profits tax in preference to that.

FORD: I'm not sure I understand the difference between a windfall and an excess-profits tax.

SIMON: Sir, the windfall tax aims like a rifle at crude oil, as opposed to an excess-profits tax, which would cut across the whole range of an extremely complex system of profit calculation.

GREENSPAN: Trying to audit through the profits system of the multinationals would lead you into a hopeless maze.

The Vice President subsides like a balloon with the air escaping.

FORD: The main thing is to attach as few amendments as possible to the tax bill, so as to get the stimulus as soon as we can. . . .

The meeting lasts for an hour and fifteen minutes and goes into great detail on issues that are quite technical: an intention to impose countervailing duties on European Community dairy products; proposed Export-Import Bank financing of liquefied natural-gas facilities abroad; negotiations with Chairman Albert Ull-man of the House Ways and Means Committee on the energy bill, and what to do about "their" $5.9-billion Emergency Employment Appropriations Act.

Mr. Rockefeller with belling tones interrupts the Ex-Im discussion with a warning that supertankers carrying liquefied gas are extremely dangerous. If one blew up in an American port, he says, the whole city would go up. He paints a vivid picture of urban devastation.

The President's interventions are minor, until the

discussion of the Democrats' big bill to provide jobs. Here his only interest is in keeping spending down. He proposes the preparation, as quickly as possible, of "an updated scoreboard" on the budget, reflecting Congressional proposals to spend more and more, and Congressional refusals to rescind or defer spending already authorized. He stresses more than once the need to dramatize "their" additions to the deficit.

Why am I shocked? Because in this discussion I have seen a first glimpse of another side of the man who has been so considerate, so open and so kind to me as an individual—what seems a deep, hard, rigid side. Talking here, he has seemed a million miles away from many Americans who have been hardworking people all their lives and are now feeling the cruel pinch of hard times. What is it in him? Is it an inability to extend compassion far beyond the faces directly in view? Is it a failure of imagination? Is it something obdurate he was born with, alongside the energy and serenity he was born with?

12:16 P.M. He takes Rockefeller into the Oval Office with him. To my regret, I am not invited to join them —I would have loved to see the Immovable Object and the Irresistible Force collide.

I gather they talk about two things. First, the Domestic Council. This body, originally conceived as a planning unit in the Executive, devolved under Nixon and Ehrlichman into an operational clearinghouse that kept things moving. Ford and his staff early saw a need to restore its predictive function, because it was obvious that the President was not by nature a planner. Ford had had a long habit of juggling a multiplicity of problems in the Congress that demanded instant attention; everything was always on a day-to-day basis. And he succeeded to the Presidency, as his Counsel Philip Buchen puts it, "under a tyranny of urgency." And much as he would have liked to emulate Truman, he lacked Truman's sense of history—lacked a feel for how a decision would look five—or fifty—years hence. The thought was that Rockefeller, having put a Commission on Critical Choices to work after he resigned from the Governorship of New York, might bring a planning competence to the council. Ford appointed James M. Cannon, long a political adviser to Rockefeller, as director of the council, and the two men talk now about the early stages of Cannon's and the council's work.

Second, the C.I.A. Who should investigate?

12:35 P.M. The President calls in Alan Greenspan to fill him in on the conversation yesterday with Dr. Burns. Alan Greenspan is a devotee of Ayn Rand (*The Fountainhead, Atlas Shrugged*), the Objectivist philosopher, and, like her, he advocates pure *laissez-faire* capitalism and "rational selfishness."

12:46 P.M. General Scowcroft goes in for two minutes— presumably with the latest word from Dr. Kissinger.

12:48 P.M. Mr. Ford receives Frank Stanton, former vice chairman of the board of CBS, who for a year and a half has chaired a panel, set up jointly by the U.S. Advisory Commission on Information and the U.S. Advisory Commission on International Education and Cultural Affairs, reviewing the operations of the U.S. Information Agency, the Voice of America and the Bureau of Cultural Affairs of the Department of State.

Before each appointment, the President is given what is formally called a briefing paper; informally, a talking paper. It has three parts: a statement of the purpose of the appointment, background and "talking points"—actual language the President might appropriately use.

In this instance, Mr. Ford has been given the following talking points:

"(1) I understand that your panel has addressed some of the long-standing issues. . . . These activities play an important role. . . .

"(2) There have been a number of proposals in recent years for restructuring our information and cultural activities. . . ."

Mr. Stanton is then to be given a chance to make his recommendations—which, in the event, are that U.S.I.A.'s information functions be transferred to the State Department, that the long-range cultural functions of U.S.I.A. and State be combined within State and that the Voice of America be set up as an independent entity under a Government-and-public board.

"(3) The scope of your study and its recommendations are very impressive. I will want to have it studied very carefully. . . .

"(4) Thank you for your efforts. . . . You have made a most needed and timely contribution."

Actually, the exchange is far freer and a little less grammatical than this, but, all the same, it's the way it goes.

1:10 P.M. The President retires for lunch. I join him for a few minutes in his two-room hideaway. One room is a small study, the walls of which are covered with mementos, including a huge Presidential seal which is

actually a rug, hooked for the President in Grand
Rapids by his half-sister-in-law, Mrs. Richard Ford; in
one corner there is a luxurious stuffed-leather Barca-
lounger, into which the President occasionally settles
to read.

His lunch is served on a tray on a small table beside
a desk in the other room.

Day in and day out, Mr. Ford eats exactly the same
lunch—a ball of cottage cheese, over which he pours
a small pitcherful of A-1 Sauce, a sliced onion or a

quartered tomato, and a small helping of butter-pecan ice cream.

"Eating and sleeping," he says to me, "are a waste of time."

I tell him that it has appeared to me that he likes being President.

"I do," he says. "It's mainly the challenge, John. I always have enjoyed facing up to problems; it's always been a sort of way of life with me—and you certainly have them here. I really enjoy getting up every morning, looking at the schedule, seeing what the problems are. I don't long for the end of the day."

2:03 P.M. Secretary of Defense James Schlesinger and General Scowcroft are closeted with the President, to report on the deteriorating situations in Cambodia and Vietnam. After about half an hour, I am admitted.

They are talking about G.I. Bill education, which the President apparently wants to cut back, or perhaps cut out altogether. The tall, rugged-looking Secretary holds the line as well as he can.

FORD: You do get into a paradoxical situation. You have an all-volunteer service, but these benefits give an incentive to get out.

SCHLESINGER: They give an incentive to get in, sir. But many will stay. We're attracting a different sort of person.

FORD: Ever thought of offering a greater educational opportunity if they stay in?

SCHLESINGER: We do some of that now, Mr. President, but we're going to cut back on it. English grammar but not basket weaving, for which they've gotten credit in the past.

49

. . . with Schlesinger and John Hersey in the background

FORD: There are things I can do to cut off certain benefits. But we'll have to go to Congress sooner or later. There has to come a time when we end the so-called Vietnam war and all its extras.

SCHLESINGER: We'll get up an options paper on the whole thing.

The two now discuss several other subjects—officers' pay, certain personnel decisions, Thailand, Diego Garcia, Turkey.

Suddenly the President leans forward, and with a vigor far surpassing any I have previously seen him show, his voice rising almost to a shout, his forefinger pounding on the edge of the desk, he adjures the Secretary to get the Navy going on the Elk Hills petroleum reserve.

FORD: Get up there and get the legislation, or we're going to give that whole deal to Interior. Tell 'em to get off their cushions up there at the Navy. The Navy damn well better get moving. I want you to get action. It strikes me the Navy likes the cushy little deal they've got out there. I'm going to go and see Elk Hills, and when I come back I'm going to be one of the few people who's actually seen the place, and I'm going to be in a position to tell 'em what's what. Now you get going.

SCHLESINGER (*to his Commander in Chief*): Yes, sir.

3:08 P.M. Rumsfeld, Cheney and William N. Walker, Director of the Presidential Personnel Office, come in to talk about some prospective appointments.

4:20 P.M. Marsh, Cheney, Cabinet Secretary James Connor and Dr. Robert Goldwin enter to warm Mr. Ford up for the *Fortune* interview. Dr. Goldwin has recently been appointed a consultant, with a mission of bringing intellectuals in to see the President. So far, he has exposed Ford to people like Irving Kristol, of the Department of Urban Values, New York University; Gertrude Himmelfarb, historian, of City College, New York; Thomas Sowell, an eminent black economist, of U.C.L.A.; Herbert Storing, a political scientist, of the University of Chicago; and Edward Banfield, an urban specialist, of the University of Pennsylvania.

In preparation for this meeting, Dr. Goldwin has provided Mr. Ford with the *Encyclopedia of American History*, edited by Richard B. Morris *et al.*, and the *Encyclopedia of American Facts and Dates*, edited by Gorton Carruth, with certain pages tabbed. Mr. Ford has done his homework. There is a meandering conversation on history—one which Mr. Truman would never have needed; or, had he heard it, would have called just too damned highfalutin.

4:55 P.M. *Fortune* editors in. Goes pretty well, Mr. Ford reports afterward.

5:40 P.M. Marsh, Friedersdorf, Cannon, Cheney, Lynn, Lynn's O.M.B. deputy, Paul O'Neill, and a couple of other staff members meet with the President to discuss the possibility of sending a message to Congress on a consumer-protection bill.

Once again, as the group reviews a long options paper, I hear in the President's comments the distant, hard-edged, negative voice I heard this morning in the economy-energy meeting.

FORD: Is a consumer-protection bill in any form a violation of our new policy of limited spending?

LYNN: You're going to get a new law, no matter what

you put in this. It's almost a certainty they'll have a law.

FORD: Then you get a question: Is it wise for me to go with a message?

LYNN: Well—to get out in front with the consumer. . . .

FORD: On page two, we ought to hold this for further study. . . . I'd be very hesitant about establishing a consumer-representative office in every department. Your agency head is going to lose control. . . . We ought to get better titles for things. The Democrats come up with titles like Model Cities, and we come up with the Ocean Dumping Act. . . . (*Considerably later, after discussion of nineteen of twenty-four options:*) I must say, on the basis of what we've been talking about, I can't see justification for sending up a message on consumer protection. . . .

In the end, Marsh suggests that at a Cabinet meeting the President might "mandate the departments to concern themselves with consumer considerations." The President adds that he might then also write letters to the chairmen of the appropriate committees, on the need for certain reforms in the regulatory agencies.

So much for the faraway consumer.

6:55 P.M. Rumsfeld and Cheney come in together for the evening cleanup. At one point:

RUMSFELD: This is just something to think about. It occurred to me after our meeting this morning with Ron [Nessen] that began as a session where he could get guidance from you, and then the Congressional side came in, so Max [Friedersdorf] could get guidance, then other voices were added, so that now it has become a kind of senior staff meeting. This morning it was scheduled for fifteen minutes and lasted an hour.

FORD: This morning the circumstances were rather special.

RUMSFELD: That's true. That's true. But what I'm wondering is whether there shouldn't be a regular senior staff meeting in place of that. And whether we shouldn't get in a somewhat different cast of characters—Jim Lynn, Brent, Jack, Bob. It's fine for Ron to come to you and get your position on things, beyond which he wouldn't go.

FORD: As long as he could get some input from you and others besides myself—

RUMSFELD: Sure. He does that all day every day. . . . Maybe the senior staff meeting should be followed by a smaller group in here with you.

CHENEY: Or perhaps you should preside over the senior staff group.

FORD: Always remembering that I get more out of a meeting with several people than just one.

RUMSFELD: I'm just thinking of the most efficient use of your time.

FORD: Why don't you think it through and come up with a plan?

7:20 P.M. Mr. Ford leaves for the residence. Today he spent four minutes less in his office than yesterday.

WEDNESDAY

Politics: "That's How It Works"

7:38 A.M. Here he comes along the walkway through another soggy dawn. He steps through a tall door into the brightness of the office in a newish three-piece suit, middling brown with a faint check, trousers cuffless, and when he bends down over the brown suitcase for some papers and then swings quickly toward his desk chair, coattails flying, you can see that the pattern of his silk foulard tie, riding a sliver of a tie pin, is repeated in the lining of the jacket. He has no less than three pens clipped in the vest pocket over his heart. The Presidential seal helps link his white cuffs.

Like everyone else in the vicinity, I am energized by the zest of this arrival. I feel the need of a lift. Some bad questions have been building in my mind. Whatever became of the motto of "communication, concilia-

55

tion, compromise and cooperation" with the Congress that the President promised on the Monday after his swearing-in? Why does everything here seem to present itself in terms of a contest with "them"? Yet when he loses and "they" win a round in that struggle, why is he so quiet, so unperturbed, as if nothing really has been lost—suggesting that nothing would have been gained, either, if he had won? What is the source and nature of the deep, hard sound I heard in this kind man's voice yesterday, the sound that troubled me so?

7:42 A.M. General Scowcroft and David Peterson, of the C.I.A. White House Support Staff, go in for the daily briefing.

8:02 A.M. Counselor Hartmann goes in for his daily appointment.

But this morning I go to the senior staff meeting in a sort of mini-Cabinet room, where Teddy Roosevelt glares down exultantly from over the mantel at the bully young chaps he sees at the long table. Ford's staff, befitting his constant yearning to be with friends, is horizontal in form. Nixon's was pyramidal; urgencies mounted the slopes to Haldeman at the apex, and then went in, maybe. Nine men of Ford's staff can walk into the Oval Office at any time—though there are obviously heavy constraints on their doing so: Assistant Rumsfeld, Assistant Kissinger (or Scowcroft), Counselor Marsh, Counselor Hartmann, Press Secretary Nessen, Counsel Buchen, Assistant (Economy) Seidman, Assistant (Budget) Lynn, Assistant (Domestic Council) Cannon. The senior staff comprises these men, and they or their deputies, and some others, like

Frank ("the Energy Zarb") Zarb, Greenspan and Friedersdorf, attend. Secretary Simon is sometimes present, though not today.

Rumsfeld sits at one end of the long table, and he calls on one man after another. Whoever has something on his mind that he thinks the President either should know or should act upon speaks his piece; others take passes.

Budget's Lynn says that yesterday he took the liberty of telling some reporters that the Democrats' $5.9-billion emergency spending bill would overstimulate the economy and swell the deficit, and that he would urge the President to veto it; perhaps some of the staff have seen the story in this morning's *Post*.

Several have. There is some talk about "how high a profile" the President should have on vetoes at this stage of delicate bargaining. Up to this morning, he has vetoed twenty-five bills—has been the most veto-prone President since Grover Cleveland, the all-time record holder. Most of his vetoes have been standing up recently, however, and, indeed, Friedersdorf now reports that yesterday the Democratic leadership decided it did not have the troops to override Mr. Ford's veto of the ninety-day oil-tax delay.

"Just thought I'd toss out a signal to them," Lynn says.

Friedersdorf tells the staff he has some other good news, too, for a change—that the Senate Foreign Relations subcommittee dealing with emergency aid to Cambodia yesterday voted 4 to 3 in favor of giving the Cambodians $125 million, and a House Foreign Affairs subcommittee split 3 to 3 on a proposal for somewhat less aid; the Cambodian proposition is not dead. . . .

• • •

8:40 A.M. In the Oval Office.

RUMSFELD: The slot situation. As you know, we've been keeping periodic book on how we're doing on the 10-percent reduction in the White House staff. We now have 533 permanents. We're aiming for 490, although we budgeted 500 for some leeway. It's very hard; there's constant pressure to add people. Last month we had seventeen departures and thirteen arrivals. We have a sizable percentage to reduce between now and June.

FORD: You'll just have to keep the pressure on.

RUMSFELD: We should be thinking about the problem of coordinating domestic and foreign policies. This has been a problem in our Government since the forties, at least. On that business yesterday of the countervailing duties on European cheese and so on, Simon went ahead on the basis of domestic pressures—no contact with State, which has to deal with the repercussions in the European Economic Community. Something to think about. . . .

9:00 A.M. One of Counselor Marsh's many duties is as White House overseer of plans for the Bicentennial in 1976. On the way in to his appointment, Marsh, a Virginian chauvinist, whispers to me that he thinks of the whole forthcoming celebration not as Bicentennial but as Tercentennial—on account of Bacon's Rebellion against the Virginian colonial authorities in 1676.

MARSH (*to the President*): They're getting ready to go with a Wagon Train, a Freedom Train—all sorts of national programs, some O.K., some awful. The workload on the Bicentennial is getting pretty fierce, Mr. President, and I wonder if we could set up a task force on it? I'd suggest [Human Resources Assistant] Marrs,

Cheney, Goldwin, [Cabinet Secretary] Connor, [Domestic Council Director] Cannon.

FORD: Good idea.

MARSH: Each state will have one week of national observance, with one night each in the Kennedy Center. With fifty states, that'll take just about the whole year. It's an idea that might suit me, but it sure might not suit you. Once a week!

FORD: The only thing that would suit you would be a thirteen-week celebration, for the original thirteen colonies. Right?

MARSH: Of which Virginia, sir, was the first. Do you know that until 1937 Virginia was a colony longer than she was a state?

FORD: Some think longer than that.

MARSH: We've got to work out a role for you that won't pull you apart. . . . The 1876 Centennial theme was technology. Alexander Graham Bell introduced the telephone, up in Philadelphia, I think it was. There was the reciprocating engine. New processes. Men came on from St. Louis and Akron and Council Bluffs, and there was a great outward burst in technology. We need to get some sort of logos built into our planning.

FORD: Jack Stiles [co-author of *Portrait*] was talking to me about the idea of getting an American electronic and aviation and space-industry show set up at Cape Canaveral. They've got a lot of unused space down there since the cutbacks.

MARSH: A sophisticated Disneyland. That's a good idea.

FORD: I think it's a meritorious idea. . . .

9:19 A.M. Most of the discussion in the Nessen group this morning is political. Max Friedersdorf's slightly encouraging news from the Hill raises questions: how to push through as much Cambodian aid as will survive; how to get Congress to move on the tax bill; how to get "their" big-spending bill recommitted.

The President stirs with pleasure—it almost seems as if he has suddenly walked through a door into his real self. Familiar names: the old horse-trading routines. Even his hands seem independently to enjoy themselves now as they settle into the little enactments of bargaining they know so well—counting, weighing, arresting; a finger encircles a thumb (We have that man), knuckles rap the desk (Try again), the whole hand flaps (He's hopeless), reminiscences about motions to recommit like memories of great football games. The names like candies in his mouth: Frank, Gale, Hugh, John, Al, Herman, Gaylord, Barber, Mike. . . .

FORD: That Gale McGee is a stanch guy. I remember when Gale and I used to fight tooth and nail for foreign appropriations. In those days, old Passman was adamant against anything foreign. . . . What's the next step, Max?

FRIEDERSDORF: Well, the House subcommittee will vote again, of course, and the full Senate committee will vote, I believe, on Monday.

FORD: Anything I can do?

FRIEDERSDORF: Our present count on the probable vote in the full Senate committee is seven to seven, with Senator Percy undecided. I think a call to the Senator would be most helpful.

FORD: Sure, I'll call Chuck.

JACK HUSHEN (*Nessen's deputy, who is going to have to take the briefing this morning, because Nessen will be sitting in on a scheduled Cabinet meeting*): What am I to say about this Republican loyalty oath, to you and the principles of the party, that Representative Anderson and Senator Percy are circulating? A kind of pledge of allegiance to the party.

FORD: Haven't seen it. I only saw the news story.

FRIEDERSDORF: John Anderson mentioned it Monday night.

RUMSFELD: A value it does have is that it brings people out into the open, and it offsets that Rhodes stuff about a program independent of yours.

FORD: Let's say I'm grateful for this show of strong support—

HARTMANN (*always the realist*): You don't have that yet.

FORD (*trying again*): I'm grateful for the support, and I hope as many as possible—

MARSH: "Loyalty oath" is not what it is.

FORD: I wouldn't use that term at all.

FRIEDERSDORF: Or even "vote of confidence." . . .

HUSHEN: Jim Lynn came out in the papers urging you to veto the big emergency jobs bill. Do you want to say something about that?

FORD: I do feel an inclination to veto a bill for $5.9 billion. But I don't want to get too far out in front on that, because some of these smart politicians up there might tack onto the bill something we want a lot—this Cambodia and Vietnam aid. This word of warning from Jim Lynn, Director of O.M.B.—that's a pretty strong signal. That's as far as I'd want to go just now. . . .

9:46 A.M. Mr. Ford reads some briefing papers—Cabinet meeting coming. Across the room, the Seymour grandfather clock utters, utters, utters. . . .

· · ·

10:17 A.M. The President goes to the Cabinet Room to greet fifty-three state and national winners of the twenty-eighth annual Voice of Democracy scriptwriting contest, sponsored by the Veterans of Foreign Wars and its Ladies' Auxiliary, for which, this year, half a million competing tenth-, eleventh- and twelfth-grade students across the country have written short broadcast scripts on the theme "My Responsibility as a Citizen."

As the Chief Executive enters, these young presences fill the Cabinet Room with a vibrant energy, like that of a ravenous school of fish breaking water to feed. They surge forward, wink flashbulbs, blurt out heartfelt encouragement and advice. The President's cool soon quiets them.

Mr. Ford's talking paper has offered him some bland suggestions on how to greet these winners: "I want to thank . . . congratulate . . . I would like to hear each one of you. . . ."

Instead he strikes out on his own with a brief and basic civics lesson—so basic as to be, it seems, quite a few grade levels below those of his audience; yet he delivers the central passage of this simple lecture with an intensity of emotion that I have not heard in anything he has said up to this time:

FORD: I think this is a wonderful thing for the V.F.W., of which I am a member, and its Ladies' Auxiliary, to have done. You've been here for a week? Then I trust you've seen all three branches of the Government. This Government of ours has three coequal branches. First we have the Supreme Court, that's the first branch. Then the Senate and the House of Representatives, that's the second. And then we have the President and the Executive Branch, that's the third. We have a system of checks and balances. The founders of this Government, those who drafted the Constitution, had very strong feelings that the best way to protect individual freedom and to meet the challenges from day to day was to keep this system of checks and balances in each branch strong—and also to leave substantial powers in the hands of state and local governments. I hope you'll go back to your states and sooner or later you'll take some part in one of these branches, whether in the Judiciary, or as a Senator or Congressman, or maybe right here as President. Have a safe trip home, and we'll see you back here one of these days, hopefully, running things.

·   ·   ·

10:22 A.M. General Scowcroft and Rumsfeld confer with the President in the Oval Office.

10:45 A.M. Mr. Ford spends a quarter of an hour preparing himself for the Cabinet meeting. 11:04 A.M.— The President enters the Cabinet Room. 11:05 A.M.— "Camera Opportunity": Photographers bustle and shove. 11:07 A.M.—Exit press.

11:08 A.M.
FORD: We have a very full plate today, and we should get started.

Rumsfeld talking to O'Neill, Rockefeller and Coleman in the background

He greets two new Secretaries, Carla Hills of HUD and Bill Coleman of Transportation, and reserves time for a departing Secretary, Peter Brennan of Labor, to speak at the end of the meeting.

He tells the Cabinet that with the extension of the Clemency Board's period of activity, there has come a sudden flood of 11,000 new applications for clemency from draft evaders and A.W.O.L.'s, with 4,000 to 5,000 more cases expected before the deadline. To save money on the huge load of clerical work this will entail, he asks all the departments to lend staff personnel to the Clemency Board.

Now he calls on Vice President Rockefeller to give the Cabinet an account of the recent drama in the Senate over the filibuster, during which the Vice President, in a handsome display of Rockefeller gall, faced down the Southern bloc and brought about a long-needed and historic change in the rules of procedure, under which 60 percent of the Senate, rather than, as in the past, two thirds, could henceforth vote to limit debate—thus curbing the power of a regressive minority to resist change simply by talking a bill to death. "I might add," Ford says, "that Rocky handled himself brilliantly."

The Vice President rises, brimming with joy, and Dick Parsons, a towering assistant of his, props up a large chart on an easel at the end of the room, and hands Mr. Rockefeller a wooden pointer.

ROCKEFELLER: . . . On January 10, I asked the President how he wanted Rule 22, which regulates filibusters, handled. The President decided that as the presiding officer of the Senate, it was my responsibility and that I should handle it as I saw fit. As you can see by the chart, there are essentially two strategies, referred to as the Northern and Southern routes. . . . Mondale put two motions in one during this period, which is incorrect, and that was disallowed. Then Senator Allen put three motions in one, which was also disallowed. Senator Byrd and Senator Griffin finally agreed on the wording of the motion, but Mansfield objected. . . . As we moved through these series of steps outlined on the chart, alternating between the Northern and Southern routes and various motions, we reached a point where I asked for the clerk to call the roll. Senator Allen objected and raised a point of parliamentary inquiry. The Vice President again then asked for the roll to be called, and again Senator Allen raised the point of question of parliamentary inquiry and again I asked for the roll to be called. This is where the controversy really became a public feud. The Senators at that point gave me a very bad time. But according to Rule 19 in the Senate, on a point of parliamentary inquiry the Chair is allowed, at his discretion, to recognize or not recognize the Senator. At any rate, we finally reached an agreement. There was a two-hour recess during which a compromise was worked out, and the final agreement was the Southern route, which is the way the majority wanted to go. Everyone was happy—the conservatives, the liberals, the Republicans and the Democrats have all generally turned out to be fairly happy about it. I have arranged a series of small dinners with various members of the Senate to make certain that there are no hard feelings. . . . I might add, Mr. President, that I am grateful for the support that you gave me during this period, both publicly and privately. I appreciate it, and I believe and hope I did what you wanted. . . .

FORD: At this time, I would like Earl Butz to tell us

what has been happening to farm and food prices, and what we can expect for the rest of the year. Earl?

BUTZ: Well, Mr. President, it looks like this. There has been a 14-percent increase in price of food in 1974 over 1973. Eighty percent of that increase has come after the product has left the farm. This can be accounted for by higher wages, higher transportation costs and higher fuel costs. While the increase has slowed down some, it has not stopped during the first quarter of 1975. It appears that food prices will be up 1½ percent to 2 percent over the last quarter of 1974. So the increase has slowed down markedly. It is interesting to note that the index of prices paid by farmers is up 12 percent, but the index of prices received by farmers is down by about 15 percent. The statistic that you will find interesting is that 17 percent of the take-home pay of the average American will go for food. This is down slightly over 1973, and also interesting to note is that only Canada and the United States are nations below 20 percent of take-home pay going for food. This can be attributed to several things. One-third of the meals are currently eaten outside of the home. Looking toward 1975, we anticipate a leveling off or decline in food prices. There will be more beef eaten by Americans this year by about seven pounds per capita for the year. However, Americans will eat less pork and poultry per person, and the beef will be relatively cheap. Fruits and vegetables will generally be less expensive, and of course, Mr. President, you know about our peanut problem. We have had one for years. We are up to our ears in peanuts. The area where we will be shortest in everyday diets will be on grain-fed beef. Mr. President, you can expect a record wheat crop. Since 70 percent of all wheat in America is winter-grown, that crop is already in. We have had a 6-percent increase in acreage, and 400 million to 500 million bushels of grain above last year's crop, so we will have a record crop. We currently have four million acres in soybean cultivation. So we hope, as we look toward 1975, the escalation of food prices is behind us.

FORD: Are the farmers happy, Earl?

BUTZ: No, sir, they aren't.

Now the President introduces Administrator Russell Train of the Environmental Protection Agency to explain a controversial decision Mr. Train made last week, giving the automobile industry until 1978 or even—if Congress will approve—until 1982 to meet final antipollution standards.

TRAIN: Thank you, Mr. President. As most of you know, it was a very complicated and controversial issue. . . . As you know, autos using catalytic converters cut down pollutants, give low operating costs, better gas consumption and have fewer maintenance problems; but it has been found that they also give sulphuric-acid mist, which is dangerous. So the decision was whether to hold the line and continue with the interim standards, or to go with the higher standards and run the risk of putting the sulphuric-acid mist in the air. Our research indicated that the sulphuric acid was a very real and dangerous problem. While it isn't a national problem yet, it soon could be, and we really can't afford to play the numbers game. Through our research we found that desulphurization was not a good solution, for it would take some two years of research and testing to be prepared to do that on a regular basis. We also found that sulphate traps aren't a solution, and not something that our technology is readily able to produce. The real concern we had was

Clockwise from the President: *Schlesinger, Hills, Butz, Secretary of Commerce Frederick B. Dent, Rockefeller, Attorney General Edward H. Levi, Brennan, Buchen, Deputy Secretary of State Robert S. Ingersoll* Far wall: *Hersey, Scowcroft, Friedersdorf, Zarb, Parsons*

if we moved to the new higher level of standard, which is the .9 California standard, we would actually be doubling the amount of sulphuric acid in the air. Therefore, after much thought and a lot of advice, the decision was made to stay with the 1975 interim standard, 1.5 percent hydrocarbons as opposed to .9 percent, the California standard. This of course caused considerable problems. The health-services industry was not happy, the auto people were not happy, and the Mayors and Governors were not happy.

There is considerable discussion of the catalytic-converter issue. Vice President Rockefeller, having had a nice chance to talk, is relatively unbouncy today, but soon he does sound another of his alarms.

ROCKEFELLER: Mr. President, I fear that this could really become a serious political problem and perhaps a liability next year. I know we will have examples of garages catching on fire and people burning to death; cars catching on fire, gas stations exploding—all because of the catalytic converter. If someone wanted to make this a political issue in 1976 and brought out these gruesome details and stories, they would put the burden on your back, and they would be asking why you didn't tell them that this was a problem. . . .

TRAIN (*later*): Mr. Vice President, what you say is true, perhaps, to a certain extent, and if one carried it to the extreme, it could become a political liability. However, the reports about fires, explosions and death are very fragmented at best. We simply don't have adequate information at this time to prove that this is true. If we do pull the catalyst off the automobile at this time, we will have an increase of three times in the level of pollutants.

ROCKEFELLER: I would really like to see the President take the public into his confidence and include them in this information, so they feel like they are sharing in the decisions, and we can assist them in making their determinations, and this therefore will not become a political liability at a future date. . . .

FORD (*after twenty minutes' discussion*): Last October we decided that an inflation-impact statement should be made about all new legislation which we were proposing and the Congress was proposing. Maybe we can do the same thing here. It says something about my basic philosophy of government. I think that we have to implement this philosophy, and the consumer has a right to know what the exact impact, both pros and cons, will be of decisions which his Government is making. It's not just environmental regulations that raise this issue. There are literally thousands of examples. I recall the problem we had with the truckers' regulation issued by the Department of Transportation before you arrived, Bill. I had to make a decision on New Year's, when I was on vacation, to let a regulation go forward because we were so far down the road on it. To hold it up would have imposed economic hardship on the industry, which had geared up to implement the Federal rule. As a result, we are increasing the cost of trucks and trailers 5 to 7 percent—it's some very large sum like 200 million dollars. I now understand that this regulation might force some companies out of business. I have no doubt that many energy regulations create the same kind of dislocations. Therefore, when we submit legislation and proposals, we must make certain that we know both sides of the story and what the total impact will be, so we can inform the Congress and the public about everything to do with that particular problem.

Next the President calls on Secretary Schlesinger to brief the Cabinet on the situation in Cambodia and Vietnam.

The Secretary unwraps maps; there is some joshing, to the effect that he might simply use Rocky's filibuster chart, which is still on the easel, to make his case.

The Secretary's briefing, the discussion that follows it, and Secretary Brennan's swan song, uttered in the street-hardened tones of Hell's Kitchen, Manhattan, conclude the meeting.

12:44 P.M. The President returns to the Oval Office for a chat with Secretary Morton. They discuss Morton's imminent transfer from Interior to Commerce.

71

12:58 P.M. Mr. Ford is joined by Congressmen John Rhodes and Albert H. Quie for a short prayer meeting. Mel Laird usually joins the group in these habitual devotions, which have continued intermittently for about seven years; he is unable to be present today. The three talk awhile, then each prays aloud and alone for about a minute, asking for guidance, giving thanks, weaving in his largest concerns, praying not only for his own interest or for those of the President, but also for the good of Congress and the country. Then the three intone the Lord's Prayer together.

1:10 P.M. Lunch: cottage cheese drenched in A-1 Sauce, and so forth. 1:20 P.M.—Mildred Leonard, Mr. Ford's executive secretary for twenty-three years, comes into the hideaway to assist him with private correspondence. 1:35 P.M.—Other paperwork. 1:57 P.M.—Major Robert E. Barrett, one of the President's military aides, in for three minutes on a personal errand.

2:03 P.M. For the third time today, the President enters the Cabinet Room, this time to receive the United States Commission on Civil Rights.

Chairman Arthur Flemming, former Secretary of Health, Education and Welfare, has asked for this meeting to discuss the current state of Federal enforcement of civil-rights law. The President has done his homework, and shows his familiarity with many of the questions Chairman Flemming and other commission members raise. It does not take him long to start talking about Congress:

FORD: Of course you know that I have recommended a five-year extension of the voting-rights law. We may have a problem up there on the Hill. You know the present act expires August 8. I've noted that several interested and influential members of Congress think something ought to be added to the act for the benefit of Spanish-speaking citizens; others want to extend the act to some pockets in the North where you have alleged discrimination; others want to extend it to the whole country. I don't know what the impact will be, but these are knowledgeable and influential Senators and Congressmen. There could be a delay. There are some people who don't want any voting-rights law at all, and there are some who want it amended. If those two groups got together fortuitously, you could have trouble—you might not have the present law extended. . . .

2:42 P.M. The President makes his telephone call to Senator Percy.

FORD (*leaning back*): Hi, Chuck . . . I'm fine, how're you? . . . No. Say, I appreciate the initiative you and John Anderson and Bill Milliken have taken to support me up there, trying to get a few signers here and there. . . . Oh gee, that's good, I hadn't heard that. . . . You know, it's good to have a policy, but if you don't have 51 percent of the vote! (*Laughs.*) . . . Chuck, the reason I called, in addition to thanking you, was because of the vote that's coming up Monday, I believe it is, on Cambodia in the Foreign Relations Committee. You know about the four-to-three support we got in the subcommittee for a $125-million drawdown for economic and military support. . . . I'm hoping that if, after you've looked at it, you can see your way to help out in the full committee. It would be extremely appreciated. . . . Chuck, I can't ask for anything more. . . . I have not talked to—say, while I have you, I'm sure you're cognizant of the thing Jim Pearson and Frank Church . . . Yes, the three-year program, with termination, *vis-à-vis* South Vietnam. If we could satisfy both Frank as well as Jim, this might be a way of, if we can get them to agree . . . You're a friend of Jim Pearson —could you see if you can . . . Let us know, and we'll do our best to cooperate. . . . (*Big laugh.*) I can't disagree with that under any circumstances. . . . O.K., Chuck. Right. . . . Right. . . . That's good. Many, many thanks. Good-by.

He hangs up. He turns to me and says: "That's the way it works."

I remark that it sometimes sounds to me as if he misses the good old days in Congress.

FORD: When you've worked in a place twenty-five years you can't help missing the people—on both sides. It's different. Up there you're only one of 435. Even if you're a leader, you have to work with 434 very independent people. They can tell you no, and you can't do anything about it. Down here, the President is the final decision maker on a few things, but you still have to work with those people—in a different relationship. My only ambition in all those years was to be Speaker of the House. Obviously that was not going to be. So now I'm here. I liked that, and I like this. I'm adaptable, I guess.

"That's the way it works." Suddenly, after this phone call, I have a sense of links—of a kind of chain that has been there all morning. Nostalgia about votes to recommit. "Strong feelings" about checks and balances, in the homily to the kids. "My philosophy of government"—in the Cabinet meeting—which seemed to come down to making sure the consumer understands "both pros and cons." Offering up prayers with his old friend John Rhodes—the very man who has just announced the plan for a House Republican legislative program independent of his. Doubts about survival of the voting-rights act in the give-and-take of the Hill—"knowledgeable and influential men." And now the phone call: "Chuck, I can't ask for anything more."

The adversary process of checks and balances in which Mr. Ford has become chained as President, all the more starkly because he deals with a Congress dominated by the opposition party, merely adds new links to old ones. He believes in this process. He has a long habit of playing the national poker game. It is of his essence. "I liked that, and I like this."

I go back to the press room, and someone digs out for me the text of the President's statement that Monday after the swearing-in, and I find the catch. The full sentence reads: "As President, within the limit of basic principles, my motto towards the Congress is communication, conciliation, compromise and cooperation." Now I am beginning to realize the weight of the reservation.

What are the basic principles? This morning I heard the first name Barber in passing in the Nessen session. Who is Barber? He is Barber B. Conable, Jr. And who might he be? He is the Congressman from New York who, in the last full year of Nixon's Presidency, distinguished himself by casting the greatest number of votes in favor of Nixon-backed bills of any member of Congress. For some reason Barber B. Conable, Jr., is not now President of the United States. And what about the man who *is* President? When all the ayes and nays were counted, he was the second most faithful to Nixon of all the 435 members of Congress.

The basic principles are couched in the voting record over the years: *against* Federal aid to education (1956, 1961, 1963, 1965, 1969, 1970); against Federal support for water-pollution programs (1956, 1960); against creation of the Office of Economic Opportunity (1964); against mass transit (1973); against ending the bombing of Cambodia (1973). *For* defense spending (consistently); for revenue sharing (1972); for cutting off aid to students who participated in campus disruptions (1968); for the Civil Rights Act (1964) and the Voting Rights Act (1965)—but only after the failure of weaker substitutes, which he favored; for watering down of the Voting Rights Act (1969). In 1967 he gave a speech on the House floor entitled "Why Are We Pulling Our Best Punches in Vietnam?" He supported Vietnamization. In 1970 he advocated the impeachment of Supreme Court Justice William O. Douglas.

Classical Republican conservatism is deeply implanted in Gerald Ford. The hard sound I heard yesterday was perhaps less a matter of coldness of heart than of glacial caution. Wariness in a world in which change is rampant. The aggressiveness of the defensive center —most valuable man on the team.

And, above all, I realize there is this: Ever since he entered public life in 1949, Gerald Ford has been on the losing side. He has always been a member of the minority. He has a firm habit of losing—of shrugging off each setback and of turning to the next day's hopeless task.

76

"I'm adaptable, I guess." Now I wonder, how adaptable? In form or in substance? In ways of working or the set of the mind?

3:23, 3:34, 3:49, 3:55, 4:09 P.M. The President interviews a series of candidates for replacement of his military assistant. At the end of the session Dick Cheney, Rumsfeld's deputy, asks him his preferences.

FORD: Who-all on the staff interviewed them?

CHENEY: Jack, Don, Brent, [Staff Secretary] Jerry Jones, Jim and I.

FORD: I'd rather wait and get your recommendations. (*After a pause:*) I don't want to prejudice you.

4:25 P.M. The President calls me to his desk.

FORD: I want to tell you about Bob Orben, who's coming in next. In '68 I had to represent the Republicans at the Gridiron dinner. You're supposed to be funny for ten minutes and serious for two, you know. I'd been to several of those dinners, and I'd heard two top people misjudge badly—Soapy Williams made a political speech, and John Lindsay told off-color jokes. So I thought I'd better get some help. I went to George Murphy, and he went to Red Skelton, and he got me Bob Orben, who'd been writing for TV comedians for years. Well, the speech turned out to be well received. Of course, my opposition was Hubert, and he talked for twenty-four minutes. But Bob comes in nowadays on a consulting basis. He has an excellent style, and he's broadening me out in speech work.

4:30 P.M. Orben comes in with the text for a speech the President is to make at a Gridiron-like dinner of the

Radio and Television Correspondents Association to-morrow night.

FORD (*reading aloud from the text*): "I have only one thing to say about a program that calls for me to follow Bob Hope: Who arranged this? Scoop Jackson? It's ridiculous. Bob Hope has enormous stage presence, superb comedy timing and the finest writers in the business. I'm standing here in a rented tuxedo—with three jokes from Earl Butz!"

ORBEN: I've been playing the tapes of your speeches. Your timing at the Alfalfa Club was fine—conversational. But other times you tend to be a little slow. Whenever you're doing humor, don't pause in a sentence. Watch Hope. You'll see he really punches through a line. Don't pause.

(*The President tries again.*)

ORBEN: That's better.

FORD: Is it moving?

ORBEN: You're moving right along. Put a slash in after "ridiculous." You could pause there. . . .

FORD (*a little farther on*): "And so far, this has really been a very exciting week in Washington. Particularly in the Congress. On Monday, Carl Albert picked up Bella Abzug's hat by mistake . . . put it on . . . and disappeared for three days!"

ORBEN: Very good.

FORD: If I get a laugh—would it be a good idea to gesture, as if I'm putting on a big hat?

ORBEN: I don't think it's necessary. They'll be getting a visual picture. But if you're more comfortable doing it that way—

FORD: It's a little demonstrative.

ORBEN: It wouldn't hurt.

.   .   .

5:00 P.M. Rumsfeld in the evening roundup. The astonishing range of an hour's business: the Cabinet meeting that morning; the C.I.A.; the meeting yesterday with Chief Justice Burger; the decision of the staff aides on the candidates for military assistant, and the roles, desired ranks, number and responsibilities of military aides in the future; a candidate for a Federal post; some procedural questions; the possibility of some time off for a staff member; tomorrow's schedule; a half-dozen schedule decisions for the future; some administrative questions concerning the President's secretaries; the recruiting of a new deputy for a Cabinet officer; the need for some guidance on management of an agency; Cambodia; trips that have been planned; details of an imminent visit to the West Coast; attendees at Cabinet meetings; urgent details of planning on the economy; some non-Government views on the economy; two personal matters. The President also "signs off on" the retirement of an admiral and the promotion and reassignment of two other admirals, and gives Rumsfeld three notes on matters that had come up in meetings he had had during the day, on which he wants action.

6:00 P.M. Paperwork.

7:13 P.M. To the residence.

THURSDAY

Where, Deep Down, Does the Poor Boy Lurk?

6:00 A.M. He is grinding out a mile on his exercise bike. It is a long mile, an uphill mile, because the brake screw is turned down tight. He is in navy-blue pajamas and a light-blue, short-sleeved, karate-style kimono.

"Henry exercises on one of these things," he tells me, "but while he's riding he props a book on the handlebars and reads."

We are in what can only be described, amidst the lavish décor of the rest of the White House, as the Fords' real home within the home. Mr. Ford, pumping away, tells me, "The Nixons had separate bedrooms; this used to be his." But when the Fords moved in, Betty said she and Jerry had shared the same bed for twenty-five years, and she wasn't about to let that be

81

"While Henry rides, he props a book on the handlebars."

changed. She is still asleep now in the big bed in the next room.

The President has been up since 5:30, as on most mornings. He has read part of the Washington *Post* before I arrived. He is chugging away now, his inner motor fully engaged, as alert and calm as if in a Cabinet meeting. He says he falls asleep at night in ten seconds, sleeps soundly for five hours and wakes up fully refreshed. "Oh, very occasionally," he tells me, "Betty will say, 'Gee, you had a bad night,' but I'm not cognizant of it. She'll complain I was restless. Maybe it woke her, but it didn't wake me. I sleep very deeply, and I come back easily."

He dismounts the bike and moves to a machine for strengthening thigh and knee muscles; this stands between the bicycle and a tall corner cabinet, which holds the trophies of a lifetime of competition. He sits on the red leather platform of the machine and does forty knee-lifts with each leg; on his left foot is a weight of forty pounds, on his right, twenty-five pounds. "This knee"—a hand indicates the right—"I favor a bit." Both knees suffered football injuries, and the left knee was operated on in 1932. "The other one gave me problems for thirty years," he says. "It would begin to lock on me on the fairway, or it would go weak when I was skiing. So in '72, after I got back from China, I had it operated on, too. The usual cartilage-and-ligaments thing."

He gets down on the floor and does twenty push-ups and, prone, twenty lifts of his torso, with his hands behind his head, to harden his gut.

Then, a trifle winded, he drops into a blue leather lounge chair, an old favorite of his, made in Grand Rapids, and he lifts his slippered feet onto a matching footstool and resumes reading the *Post*. "In the evenings," he says, looking over the edge of the paper, "I'll sit here, Betty'll sit there"—in an overstuffed chair close by—"and we'll read or watch television. It's just family in here." Resting on the spines of three photo albums in a magazine rack to his right, between the two chairs, is a remote-control pushbutton box for changing the channels on a television set and, under it, a paperback copy of *Plain Speaking: An Oral Biography of Harry S. Truman*, by Merle Miller. The television set is in a huge console built into the corner next to the fireplace, which is to the President's left. Beside the President's feet on the footstool is a looseleaf notebook inscribed in gold letters: *The President's Daily News Briefing*. The brown suitcase for his official papers is propped open between the footstool and the fireplace.

I leave him while he reads the rest of the paper and the staff news summary; and gets dressed.

6:55 A.M. He joins me, in shirtsleeves, and we walk into an overpowering ambiance of history in the President's dining room. The walls are papered in huge, lush and wildly inaccurate scenes of the War of Independence —Washington in command at the Battle of Niagara Falls, the capture of Wechawk Hill by Lafayette, the surrender of Cornwallis at Yorktown and Washington's triumphal entry into Boston—printed in France in 1854 by Jean Zuber. A tiny television set is on the dining table, off to the left of the President's place-setting. A scooped-out half pineapple serves as a bowl for chunks of its flesh; a tall glass of orange juice and a Thermos carafe of tea wait for him; a butler brings him a single toasted muffin with margarine. *The New York Times* is on a side table to his right, but this morning he does not read it. We eat and talk.

"I get my energy," he says, "from my mother. She was a tremendously energetic person, just fantastic. She probably had more friends than any woman I ever knew. Everybody loved her. She was a human dynamo in a womanly way. She wasn't a great career type. But she was the most thoughtful person, always writing to people—a note on a birthday—or calling on some who were in the hospital. She just had great compassion for people, plus this almost unbelievable energy."

"My very young years, I had a terrible temper," he says. "My mother detected it and started to get me away from being upset and flying off the handle. She had a great knack of ridicule one time, and humor the next, or cajoling, to teach me that anger—visible, physical anger—was not the way to meet problems. But then adversity in athletics also helped teach me. Adversity in my personal life; I thought I was madly in love with a very attractive gal. It didn't work out. One time, I thought that was the greatest catastrophe in my life. It just didn't turn out to be that way. But going back to my mother's input: She taught me that you don't respond in a wild, uncontrolled way; you just better sit back and take a hard look and try to make the best decision without letting emotions be the controlling factor."

He speaks deliberately, without emotion, sometimes pausing in midsentence to gather his thoughts, and using my first name often. He is concerned about whether I am getting enough breakfast. Dr. Lukash is very strict with him about his intake of calories, he says.

"Sometimes I do get angry," he says. "People feuding —and I guess this goes back to experiences I have had in athletics. A feuding football team never got any-place. A feuding staff in the White House is never go-ing to get anyplace. It's so senseless. Anything that's senseless is frustrating and upsets me. . . . Nothing is more frustrating to me, John, than to have staff jealousies. Nothing gets my mind off what I want to think about more than to have petty jealousies in staff people. I just can't tolerate it, and it's more disturbing to me than anything. But competence, loyalty, hard work—I do think I get those things from the people on my staff."

We talk quite a lot about football.
". . . The last game we played was with Northwest-ern, and I had a very good day against a darned good Northwestern guard. Rip Whalen. I just gave him fits. I knocked him all over the field. . . . And on the way back from the Shriners game, Andy Kerr and Curly Lambeau spent a good share of time trying to talk me into playing for the Green Bay Packers. And then Pottsy Clark, who was the head coach of the Detroit Lions, who had seen some of the Michigan games, tried to get me to play for the Lions. . . . I'd learned a little about sitting on the bench. . . . In those days, the center had to pass the ball, not to a quarterback, but to a tail-back. You really had to pass the ball; you had to lead the runner, and had to block at the same time, and you played defense, too. . . . The people that I met. . . . I

had some good teammates and good coaching, and I've kept those associations. . . . The actual competition is a pretty good character builder. . . . And football is as good a training ground from the team-operation point of view as anything I can think of. . . ."

And now he tells a strange tale. I have known that Gerald R. Ford, Jr., was not born with that name— that his mother and his actual father, then a Nebraska wool trader, were divorced when he was two years old and that not long afterward he was adopted by, and renamed for, the Grand Rapids paint salesman his mother married. The story: "I was, I think, a junior in high school in the spring, 1930. I worked at a restaurant across from South High called Skougis's. It was a 1929, 1930 hamburger stand with counters— a dilapidated place. Bill Skougis was a shrewd Greek businessman, and he hired as waiters the outstanding football players. He hired me my sophomore year. He paid me two dollars plus my lunch—up to fifty cents a meal—and I worked from eleven thirty to one, through the noon-hour class periods, and one night a week from seven to ten. I waited on table at one of the counters, washed the dishes and handled the cash register. My working place was right near the entrance. It was a long, narrow restaurant. You came in, and I was on this side washing dishes, checking people out. There was a candy counter on my side that went right down the room. There were tables and another counter. I was standing there taking money, washing dishes, and I also had to make cheese sandwiches behind the barrier. This man came in, and he stood over there. And he was a stranger. Strangers didn't come in often. This man stood over there against the candy counter. I was busy, yet I couldn't help but notice that he stood there for ten minutes. Finally he walked over to where I was working. Nobody was bothering me. 'Leslie,' he said. I didn't answer. He said, 'I'm your father.' He said, 'I'm Leslie King, and you're Leslie King, Jr.' Well, it was kind of shocking. He said, 'I would like to take you to lunch.' I said, 'Well, I'm working. I've got to check with the owner.' He said, 'I haven't seen you for a good many years. You don't know me.' So I went to Bill Skougis, and I said, 'I've got a personal matter. Will you excuse me?' And he did. My father took me out to his car, which was parked in the front—a brand-new Cadillac or Lincoln—and he introduced me to his wife. So we went to lunch. He was then living in Wyoming with his wife, and they had come out to buy a new Cadillac or Lincoln, which was a beautiful car for those days, and they had picked it up in Detroit and were driving back to Wyoming, and they wanted to stop in and see me. Which he did. And after he had finished lunch, he took me back to the school. I said good-by. He said, 'Will you come out to see me in Wyoming?' I said I'd think about it. . . . The hard part was going home that night, and how to tell my mother and step-father. That really worried me, because I had grown up, since I could remember, with my stepfather. It was only a year or two before this that I'd learned I was not living with my real father. My relationship with my stepfather was so close that it never entered my mind not to tell him. It was real hard. That was the difficult part."

"My junior year at Ann Arbor," he says, "which would be '33–'34, when my stepfather's business had long gone to pot, he was hanging on by his fingernails, my father—my real father—had been ordered at the time of the divorce to pay my mother child maintenance, and he never paid any. I was having a terrible time. Sure, I was earning my board, and I saved some money working for my stepfather in the summer. But it wasn't enough. I wasn't able to pay my bills—the fraternity, the room where I lived. And I wrote my father and asked him if he could help. And, as I recall, I either got no answer or, if I got an answer, he said he couldn't do it. I felt that, from what I understood, his economic circumstances were such that he could have been helpful. I had that impression. From that Lincoln or Cadillac I'd seen that he'd bought. And then after I graduated from Michigan, I went to Yale, of course. And then one time, out of the blue, I got a letter, a phone call, or something, saying that he was coming with his wife, the woman I had met, with his son by the second marriage—he was really my stepbrother. And they were trying to find a school in the East for him, and could they stop by and maybe I could give them some advice. So they stopped. I did meet the son. And I went to dinner with them and gave them some thoughts about schools in the East and never saw them again."

"My stepfather," he says, "was the only boy in a family of three girls. His father died at a very young age, I think of a train crash. So Dad Ford quit school, or had to—never went beyond the eighth grade. And he really lifted himself up by great effort, going step by step. He was probably one of the most respected people in the community for his civic-mindedness, his integrity, hard work. . . . He always saw something good in somebody, even people who had nothing in common with him. We got into a discussion about somebody one time, and I said, 'Oh, he's no good. He does this, or he does that.' And he said, 'Well, but he also does this, which I like—and you ought to like.' "

"At one stage," he says, "when I was eight or nine, I had a slight tendency to stutter, very infrequent, and yet it did appear once in a while. Some people alleged at that time that my being left-handed also being partly right-handed, that the ambidextrous situation contributed to the stuttering tendency. I either outgrew it or it wasn't well founded. But this is an interesting thing: I never noticed it in myself until one night I was sitting at dinner in Washington about six months ago, and this woman noticed I ate left-handed. She said, 'What else do you do left-handed?' I said, 'I write left-handed.' And she said, 'Do you throw, kick, play golf left-handed?' I said, 'No.' She said, 'You're one of the few odd people who do things left-handed when you sit down, but you're right-handed when you stand up.' I've never gone into it, but this woman really perked my interest."

"I spent a great deal of time for a period of about four years as a Boy Scout," he says. "I think scouting had a great deal to do with getting me on, and helping me stay on, some of the character attributes that I think I have, and that are important. Again, it was good associations—with leaders, with troop members. I was just very fortunate to get into a stream of athletics, student groups—a stream of people that was good, clear, strong."

·   ·   ·

He tells me another story: "As assistant navigator, I stood officer-of-the-deck watches. You had four hours on and then usually eight hours off. But it just so happened that about December 16 or 17 of 1944 we got caught in that terrible typhoon off the Philippines. We had spent the day before refueling and helping in the over-all task-force refueling operation. I had had the midnight to 0400 watch, and that was at the very high point in the typhoon. I was relieved and went down to hit the sack. And that morning I got about forty-five minutes' sleep before we had our regular morning general quarters, a half-hour before sunrise. I then went back to bed, and I had gotten back to sleep again. I don't know how long. Not very long. All of a sudden, general quarters rang again. And I woke up, and several people were dashing down the passageway yelling, 'Fire, fire, fire!'—which I later learned had been caused by a plane breaking loose, not adequately tied down, and slamming against another, and that broke loose another. And pretty soon they were all rolling back and forth as the ship rolled at the height of the storm. And, unfortunately, somebody had left some gasoline in one of the planes, and friction sparked it, and the gasoline started a fire, and these planes as they were going back and forth bashed into the air intakes, so instead of fresh air going down to the boiler room, they took in smoke from the hangar deck. So we lost ten or twelve people down in the boiler room and engine room who just never knew what hit them. . . . I woke up and I was down in officers' quarters. And I started up—have you got a pencil there? Here's the carrier, and here is the island of the carrier, right here. My stateroom with another fellow was down here. When I heard general quarters, got out of the sack, saw people running, smelled the smoke—I always went out of my stateroom up to a ladder here and then went out a door there onto the flight deck and climbed up another ladder onto the island structure to my job as officer of the deck. Well, this time, the moment I stepped out on the deck, the ship rolled way over, and I lost my balance. I went sliding just like a toboggan. Couldn't have lasted more than two or three seconds, 'cause it was only one hundred and some feet wide. But anyhow, I spread out as much as I could. There was nothing to grab on to. But fortunately around a flight deck there's a little raised metal rim so that tools won't roll over the side. And I hit that with my feet, and it spun me around, and I dropped, half in and half out of the catwalk that goes all the way around just below a flight deck. I fell halfway in and halfway out. If I'd gone another foot, I'd have gone over the side. We lost about five men overboard. For me, it was just one of those quirks. Pure happenstance. If I'd had a different angle, different speed . . ."

"You know," he says, "I wasn't married until I was thirty-five. Basically, two reasons. One, I was always so busy, never really had enough time to get involved, and I always had sort of a focus on, concentrating on something careerwise—focused in that area. And second, I had only one serious romance, other than the one I had with Betty, with this girl from Connecticut College, very superior girl—but it didn't work out. So I just forgot being too much interested in marriage. Then I met Betty, and she was very attractive. She added a sense of stability and serenity. And by the time I was thirty-five, I was pretty well on course and wasn't preoccupied. I knew where I was going—at least where I

93

wanted to try to go. And so our lives sort of fitted at that stage, plus a very excellent, broad, broad relationship. And she has done a super job, because in Congress, which our married life coincided with, she was strong, self-reliant, ran the family, gave me a chance to do things that broadened my relationships. And I think she contributed very substantially in the opportunities that materialized in my becoming President. Very loyal. She also has the capability of bringing you down to earth, once in a while, when you get some illusions. . . ."

"My gracious," he says, looking at his watch. "They'll be waiting for me."

7:42 A.M. He emerges from the family room, followed by a valet carrying the brown suitcase. In the elevator, I notice—since he now has a jacket on—that he is wearing a dark-gray double-breasted suit with peaked lapels and a hairline pinstripe. A Secret Service man is waiting at the elevator door to the ground-floor corridor. The President briskly steps out onto the dazzling crimson carpet that ties together the tunnel-like chain of Hoban's massive groined arches, which seem designed to bear all the weight of the history overhead; in the recesses of these arches, first ladies hang. Claudia (Lady Bird) Johnson is right across the way as we start along.

Standing in an open doorway on the left, opposite Caroline Scott Harrison on the right, is Rear Admiral William M. Lukash, the President's physician, who, with his almost hairless head all tanned, his figure slim and lithe, seems to have the health and poise of a hungry leopard. A specialist in gastroenterology, he was named Assistant Physician to President Nixon in 1969, and, being a Michigander with a wife from Grand Rapids, he suits Gerald Ford to a T.

"Good morning, Bill," the President says, in a tone of voice that would make it absurd to ask how he feels. The concern, at the moment, is all for Betty, who has been suffering pain this week from the mysterious pinched nerve in her neck, which has bothered her off and on for years; and for Susan, who has had a touch of bronchitis.

FORD: How's Susan? Seen her this morning?

LUKASH: Not yet. She had a little fever last night. She won't be going to school today. I'll be checking up soon.

FORD: Let me know how she is, and Betty, will you? Give me a call.

LUKASH: Yes, sir. (*Seeing me with him:*) Did you do your exercises this morning?

FORD: Yes, Doctor. Yes, Doctor.

7:44 A.M. We pace along past Edith Galt Wilson and Sarah Childress Polk, and then out into the open air —the fourth rainy day in a row—along the covered walkway beside the former swimming pool, and around into the Oval Office. Fifteen minutes late.

7:47 A.M. Scowcroft and Peterson. 8:12 A.M.—Hartmann. 8:30 A.M.—Rumsfeld. 9:07 A.M.—Marsh. 9:22 A.M.—Nessen, Hartmann, Rumsfeld, Friedersdorf. All the words the President spoke at breakfast hang like a veil of gauze over these conferences. I keep looking closely at this man who had such an energetic, compassionate mother and two fathers—or none. Are there any traces at all of the temper tantrums? Where, deep down, does the poor boy lurk, to whom two dollars a week earned at Skougis's dilapidated joint made such a difference? Nessen asks what he's to say about Scoop Jackson's proposal that Mike Mansfield go to China and negotiate with Sihanouk. This is an insolent suggestion—that the Democrats should simply take over foreign policy from the President. "The way it's being phrased," Rumsfeld says, not soothing the sting, "is, 'Why aren't you willing to try anything at this stage to get peace?'" But Gerald Ford sounds, as always, totally serene. "I frankly haven't had a chance to talk with Brent about that," he quietly says. Friedersdorf mentions the bad setback yesterday in the House, whose Democratic caucus voted 189 to 49 against any additional military aid to Cambodia. "You can say," the President calmly tells Nessen, "that my reaction was tremendous disappointment"—which does not show at all—"that such an action would be taken despite the advice of the Congressional delegation that went out to Cambodia, onto the scene."

9:57 A.M. The President leaves for a courtesy tour, long overdue, of the East Wing, where Mrs. Ford's staff, the President's Military Assistant and aides, his organization for liaison with the Hill, and those who handle White House tours and visitors have their offices. On the way through the residence, he goes upstairs to see how Betty and Susan are feeling. When he reaches the East Wing, he shakes sixty-three staff hands, ranging from that of Nancy Howe, Mrs. Ford's personal assistant, to that of the young lady who answers the not inconsiderable number of letters addressed to Shan and Liberty, the Fords' Siamese cat and golden retriever.

On the way through the open hallway to the Legislative Affairs office, he suddenly comes on a group of about fifty students and teachers from Brady Middle School, which, I am soon told, stands on Chagrin Boulevard in Pepper Pike, Ohio; this happens to be the next batch, lined up behind a barrier, for a White House tour.

"My God, it's the President!" a teacher gasps.

Mr. Ford, smiling benignly, unexcited, taking his time, walks into the group and shakes almost every hand, and asks earnest questions as he moves from one to another. The teachers are losing feathers in their flutter, but the kids take the whole scene just as calmly as he does. The news will spread like wildfire, first through Pepper Pike, then through all of Ohio, that President Ford personally greets every tour of the White House.

10:26 A.M. Back to the Oval Office. With all his leisurely motion through the morning, the President has made up the fifteen minutes of tardiness and is now five minutes ahead of schedule.

10:30 and **11:30 A.M.** The next two meetings are related to each other. The common situation is this:

The cost of postal operations has been going up. To get into the black, the Postal Service either will have to reduce its services and increase postal rates again in a few months, or will need to receive larger Federal subsidies. Wages account for 80 percent of postal costs, and one reason it has been so hard to get the Postal Service out of politics is that nearly 1 percent of the entire working population of the country is in the Postal

97

Service; there are 700,000 votes there. Postal unions will soon begin negotiating a new contract; there is talk of a possible strike, even though it would be illegal. Would the National Guard be used in that case?

The President meets first with the chairmen and ranking minority members of the House and Senate Post Office and Civil Service committees, Representatives David Henderson and Ed Derwinski, Senators Gale McGee and Hiram Fong.

McGEE: There's no way that the 30,000 post offices in this country can pay their way. We have to support them.

FORD: Could you justify a 10-percent subsidy for those communities that have post offices? . . .

McGEE: Congress doesn't think it can stand for another first-class rate increase, because we get so much mail on it. . . .

FONG: Would you designate someone on your staff for liaison with us on this?

FORD: We will do that. . . . I'd like to give the signal that we don't want a strike, we'll do everything we can to reach an equitable labor contract. But if there is a strike—well, we must move the mail. . . .

McGEE: Nobody loves us.

FORD: I'm learning that fast down here, Gale.

Meeting next with Postmaster General Benjamin F. Bailar, William J. Usery, Director of the Federal Mediation and Conciliation Service, and some others, the President gets his message across more explicitly: He believes the users of the mails should pay for the service; he does not favor larger subsidies, which, he says, would transfer costs from postal users to taxpayers at large.

Myron Wright, Vice Chairman of the Postal Board

of Governors, quietly points out that more than 8o percent of all mail is "business-oriented," and suggests
that the general public shouldn't have to subsidize
that. . . .

FORD (*toward the end of the meeting*): I want to say
very firmly, we want equity, but we can't afford to have
the inflation re-exploded. I expect the mails to be delivered. We hope the contract will be solved, but the
mails (*strong emphasis*) will be delivered.

During these discussions which have been long and
intricate, three shadowy images have been hanging
like smoke in my mind: of the junior in Deke at Ann
Arbor, unable to make ends meet, driven to begging
for money from his nonfather of a father; of the assistant navigator shooting across the tilted deck of the
Monterey and very nearly flying into the sea; of Michigan's center giving Northwestern's Rip Whalen fits,
knocking him all over the field. . . .

12:20 P.M. The President receives five-year-old Pamela
Jo Baker, the model for this year's Easter Seal poster
—a curly-haired child who has been crippled with
cerebral palsy since birth, and who has learned to walk
and talk through Easter Seal services. She wears braces
on her legs; she totters; and she seems—understand-
ably—very frightened. With her is Peter Falk, star of
the TV show *Columbo,* who is honorary national
chairman of the Easter Seal drive, her father and her
two Senators, Randolph and Byrd.

FORD (*to Falk*): My wife and I watch your program a
lot. I get very concerned about your personal security
and safety from time to time.

FALK: Don't worry about me. I'll be all right. I have to
come on the next week.

FORD: How many handicapped children do your services help?

FALK: Children and adults. Nearly 300,000 this year.

The President takes Pamela Jo up in his arms, and he talks to her softly. Then he asks where Liberty is. Somebody runs for the dog. Liberty romps wildly around the Oval Office, then suddenly lies down on her back at the President's feet.

FORD (*to Liberty*): That's not a very nice position for a lady to get into!

The President carefully pins a little brooch, with a Presidential seal on it, on Pamela Jo's dress.

When she leaves in her father's arms, the President calls, "So long, Pam." Her eyes are fearless now. She has obviously liked that quiet man who was holding her. With an effort, she waves.

12:44 P.M. General William C. Westmoreland, former commander of U.S. forces in Vietnam and former Chief of Staff of the Army, pays a call which has been deferred since early in the year because the general had a heart attack on January 5. He comes in, as it is decorously put in a briefing paper from Henry Kissinger, to "discuss his opportunities for further Government service."

FORD: I was real sorry to hear about your heart attack, Westy.

WESTMORELAND: I was the lowest-risk sort of person. No weight problem. Low cholesterol . . .

FORD: I've been trying to get Betty to go along with me on buying a place near you down there at Hilton Head, but I'm not making much progress. How's that Kuwaiti project doing? Aren't they trying to develop the shoreline near you there?

WESTMORELAND: There was some opposition from environmentalists. But now the Jews have gotten into it —some highly respected people—and I believe several houses are under construction.

FORD: Like Hilton Head?

WESTMORELAND: Smaller and more exclusive. Something like Seabrook Island.

Now, for the first time, I have noticed something. There is a certain urge toward mimicry, an echoing effect, in Gerald Ford. He seems anxious always to please; one assumes that as a basic drive in all politicians. But the hint I am getting now is of something more, some sort of protean need and knack—some part of him becomes the person he is talking with. Westmoreland sits ramrod-straight; Ford is upright now. Westmoreland talks in cranky, clipped tones; Ford is growing more spare in his speech.

. . . with General Westmoreland

FORD: I'll keep my eyes and ears open, Westy. Some part-time commission.

The President mentions one possibility—on which it is obvious the general has had his eye—but Mr. Ford says there is no vacancy. He has just replaced one person on that group.

WESTMORELAND (*taken aback*): I was given to understand there was no statutory limit on the number of members—

FORD: Well, its chairman doesn't want it to get too big. I can understand that. We'll definitely keep you in mind, though.

WESTMORELAND: I've been decorated in sixteen foreign countries. I know something about . . .

They begin to talk about conditions—about inflation and recession and energy and:

FORD: I've been having a hard time getting Congress to act responsibly on Indochina, Westy. I just learned a few minutes ago that the full House Committee on Foreign Affairs rejected the Cambodia package by a vote of eighteen to fifteen.

WESTMORELAND: It's reminiscent of the early days of the German military threat. The North Vietnamese are the Prussians of the Orient. . . . Sihanouk has no clout.

FORD: That's my impression, Westy.

WESTMORELAND: This Jackson proposal that Mansfield go out there and negotiate with Sihanouk—it's ridiculous.

FORD: Westy, they're all trying to find some way to do something that won't be enough to save the situation but'll avoid political blame. That's all there is to it.

WESTMORELAND: There is only one language that Hanoi understands, and that's force. If we'd just send our B-52's in there to bomb the supply trails and mine Haiphong harbor for a month, this whole atmosphere would change.

FORD: Unfortunately, the law says we can't do that, Westy.

2:18 P.M. Personnel Director Bill Walker and Phil Buchen in on a personnel matter.

2:35 P.M. Jim Cannon in to talk about the Domestic Council.

3:03 P.M. The President, Secretary of the Interior Morton, Lynn, Zarb, Cannon and O'Neill are disposed in sofas and chairs at the fireplace end of the Oval Office, talking about what the President calls "the politics of oil." In this case, of eking oil from the outer continental shelf, from under the sea off our shores. The question to be discussed today is not whether to drill the shelf for oil; the question is who is to get the revenues from the oil when it has been found. Maine and several other states have sued the Government, claiming they own the offshore shelf and any oil in it. Secretary Morton is to testify before the Senate Interior and Insular Affairs Committee tomorrow, and wants guidance on what to say.

What interests me in this meeting is its big-business boardroom tone—one that I have heard several times in these days. The options sound strangely corporate: "We" could take all the revenue; or, if "we" were forced to, "we" could share it with the coastal states; or, at worst, "we" might have to share it with all the states. But the Supreme Court is probably going to decide that "we" own the whole shebang.

MORTON: O.K. Let's ride this out till the Court decides.
LYNN: Let's wait, and move from a position of strength. We'd want to see what we want to buy from the states with a sharing formula.

The whole style of an Administration is revealed in the phrases that it uses. Need we hear more than "take the hang-out route" and "twisting slowly, slowly in the wind" to conjure up the entire nightmare of the Nixon decline? The style of the Ford Administration is different—it is the style of Middle American businessmen's in-group fast talk. Its root stock is Adam Smith *laissez-faire* wheeling and dealing, onto which is grafted, to produce strange fruit, the tone of voice of Eisenhower's Defense Secretary Charlie (What's good for General Motors is good for the country) Wilson. All week long I have been noting bellwether words and phrases, spoken by Cabinet members and top advisers, and I have just added three new specimens here in the outer-continental-shelf meeting. Listen:

We're going to be nickel-and-diming the multinationals. He can bring most of his Indians along. Appearancewise. Programs coming down the pike. Down the road. Downstream. Ball-park figure. They won't be able to resist matching those goodies. Paint a bigger picture. Public posture. Big go-round. Signed off on. Shopping list. They're cutting a deal up there right now. We don't want a Christmas-tree tax bill. That aims a rifle straight at crude oil. Afraid that'll tilt the industry toward the foreign car. They're trying to put some light between themselves and you. We're kind of salami-ing it. That's just putting a different gown on the same doll. Consumerism, Naderism, clean-airism. He's John Dunlop's honcho. He's going to waffle it. Pick of the litter. God-dog it. Time to get our socks pulled up on that. This could get pretty antsie-dancie in the next few weeks. I'm not married to the 5-percent figure. I'm not in glue on how far we should go. Let's be stupid, if necessary—and I find that very easy, Mr. President. A game plan and a sound signal. Let's let Hollings and Jackson fight each other till they lie down. I think I can punt tomorrow. That's one frontier that's out of the ball game. That just won't fly. Maybe you can get that under the tent. Roll it around in that direction. That's a modification I think you could hang your hat on. We'll try to screw the thing down so that it doesn't come leaking out of the basement windows.

·   ·   ·

4:07 P.M. A young Congressman from Florida named Lou Frey comes in to talk with the President about the possibility of locating a new solar-energy research program at the Kennedy Space Center, to offset recent NASA cutbacks. Frey bitterly opposed a recent 730-man cutback in personnel at Patrick Air Force Base; unemployment in the Cocoa Beach area is running about 11 percent. Frey is considered a Republican comer; he is Chairman of the Republican Research Committee in the House, and he is thinking about running against Democratic Senator Lawton Chiles in 1976. The President, after hearing his appeal, says he can't make any promises, Lou. As to the cutbacks in Lou's constituency, they've been a response to Congressional bites out of the defense budget.

Frey suddenly starts talking with flashing eyes about something called "ocean thermal gradient research," a plan for getting endless amounts of energy out of differences in temperatures in the sea. He would like to start this going in a big way off Florida, in the Gulf Stream.

FORD (*taking Frey's fire calmly*): Very interesting.

4:30 P.M. Hartmann, Theis, Friedman, Orben, Casserly come in for another session on the Notre Dame speech —into which, in the long run, the old domino theory makes its weary way.

5:25 P.M. Mr. Ford goes downstairs for a haircut; he has one every ten days or so. As Milton Pitts, the White House barber, goes to work in the brightly lit shop, the President glances at the afternoon *Star-News* and then reads over once again his gags for this evening's Radio and Television Correspondents dinner. The tex-

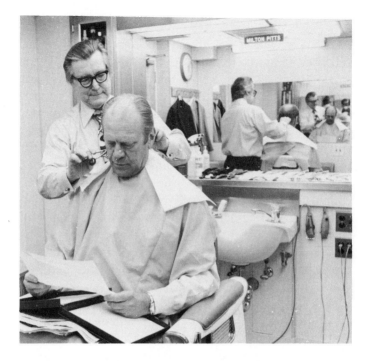

ture of Mr. Ford's hair is extremely fine; Mr. Pitts tries hard to give it the dry look, full on the sides. A quirky coincidence has brought these two men together. One afternoon about five years ago, Mr. Pitts, who operated four Washington barbershops, one of them in the Sheraton-Carlton, was approached in his Georgetown shop by a young, well-dressed man who did not sit down in a chair but asked to speak privately with him. They went into a back room. The young man said President Nixon needed a new barber—would Pitts be interested? He was. The young man was Alexander Butterfield—who, some three and a half years later, blurted out to investigators for a Senate select committee, in apparent inadvertence, that everything that took place in Richard Nixon's Oval Office was recorded on tape. It can be said that Alexander Butterfield made possible the haircut that is now taking place.

6:07 P.M. Back to the Oval Office for some paperwork.

6:15 P.M. Major General Richard L. Lawson, who is about to be replaced as the President's Military Assistant, brings his family in to say good-by.

6:24 P.M. Rumsfeld's roundup.

7:07 P.M. To the residence. Mr. Ford takes his supper on a tray on a small table in the bedroom, to be with his wife.

9:00 P.M. The President boards a motorcade on the curving driveway of the South Grounds. At 9:03 he arrives at the Statler-Hilton, where he's greeted by William W. Winpisinger, President of the Institute for Collective Bargaining, and by Postmaster General Bailar and by others. At 9:04 he pauses in a holding area outside the hotel's Congressional Room, waiting to be announced. At 9:05 he goes to the head table, where the famous labor negotiator Ted Kheel presents him with a sculpture entitled "Collective Bargaining: Out of Conflict, Accord" by George Segal, a representation of two men at a small table in head-to-head parley.

9:15 P.M. The President again boards the motorcade and rides to the Washington-Hilton Hotel. At 9:27, in the Cabinet Room of the hotel, Charlie Shutt, Washington bureau manager of Hearst Metrotone News, presents him with a can containing a sixteen-millimeter film entitled *Forward Together: Gerald Ford Assumes the Presidency.* At 9:32 the President stops by at the Jefferson Room to pay his respects to a dinner party being given by the Storer Broadcasting Company for the wives of the radio and television correspondents who are concurrently banqueting in the International Ballroom—to which, at 9:42, he proceeds. He goes to the head table. At 9:45, President Marya McLaughlin of the Radio and Television Correspondents Association introduces Bob Hope, who speaks for half an hour and is, fortunately for Mr. Ford, rather peevish and dull. At 10:23 the President begins speaking:

FORD (*he has listened carefully to Hope; he now really punches through his sentences*): I have only one thing to say about a program that calls for me to follow Bob Hope. Who arranged this? Scoop Jackson? (*An encouraging explosion of laughter.*) It's ridiculous. (*Slash —slight pause for comedy timing.*) Bob Hope has enormous stage presence, superb comedy timing and the finest writers in the business. (*Slash.*) I'm standing here in a rented tuxedo—with three jokes from Earl Butz. (*Laughter and applause!*) . . .

10:31 P.M. Remarks concluded. 10:37 P.M.—President leaves head table, goes to motorcade. 10:48 P.M.— Motorcade arrives at South Grounds.

About 11:15 P.M. The President is seated in his blue chair, feet up on the footstool, reading a long and extremely complicated briefing paper from the Domestic Council on higher education; another, also complex, is on land use.

.   .   .

Thursday

About midnight. The Iron Man goes to bed, and—if we can believe his own account, and I, for one, can, knowing at first hand that he started this day under a full head of steam 18½ hours ago and hasn't stopped once since—dives into deep, dark waters in ten seconds.

FRIDAY

But on Foreign Policy, Only Kissinger

He comes in half an hour late this morning, in a dark-blue pinstripe. The fifth rainy day in a row. He explains that he had a dental appointment on the ground floor of the residence at 7:15, and that cleaning his teeth took longer than expected. He smokes eight pipefuls of tobacco a day, he says, and that causes a lot of staining; sometimes he wishes he could cut down.

8:10 A.M. Scowcroft and Peterson go in.

I suffer now, more than the President ever seems to suffer, from a feeling of having got behind. My week as a watcher is drawing to a close, and so much that I have seen has flashed past me, as if in a speeded-up motion picture. I have a feeling of having missed many glimpses I should have been able to catch—and now, as Brent Scowcroft goes into the Oval Office, I am suddenly sharply aware of one of the unseen scenes; I have not had a single direct view, all week long, of a foreign-policy discussion, to say nothing of a foreign-policy decision.

Again this morning I attend the senior staff meeting, where I hear two suggestions put forward that exemplify the staff's efforts to grope their way, from day to day, toward efficiency.

LYNN: Every proposal to the President from a department should be tabbed with a run-down of the situation on the Hill with respect to the issue involved, and with a clear indication of what the department would intend to do on the Hill, either absent a decision from the President on the proposal, or with one. . . .

RUMSFELD: Big issues that are going to be around, and that should come before the President, should be isolated, so we make sure he has a chance to see them well ahead of time. . . .

8:55 A.M. Rumsfeld in for his morning conference.

RUMSFELD: You have meetings scheduled for the afternoon to discuss policy on land-use and higher-education legislation. O.M.B. has been trying for a long time to get the Domestic Council to prepare option papers on these areas, but with the transition in the Domestic Council to the Rockefeller crowd, it's been a bit chaotic over there, and I'm afraid they got the papers to you very late.

FORD: Do I know it! I had to wait till after the Radio-TV dinner last night to read them. Eleven thirty at night ain't a time to read up on this very complicated higher-education problem.

RUMSFELD: I'd be for no decision. Let's get an orderly look at those issues. I'll put a stop on the two meetings, and I'll set up the meeting Jim Lynn has been wanting, to talk about the no-more-spending question. . . .

9:15 A.M. Marsh goes in; after him, walking haltingly with a cane, goes the President's Counsel, Philip W. Buchen; I am uninvited to follow—and I realize that another direct view I have missed this week (because everything the Counsel touches seems to be sensitive) is that of a talk between Jerry Ford and Phil Buchen. Buchen is Ford's oldest friend and closest confidant in the White House. Three years younger than Ford, Buchen, while he was an undergraduate at Michigan, met the famous athlete at one of the house parties Delta Kappa Epsilon held each New Year's Eve in Grand Rapids; later he roomed with Ford while they both took summer courses at the Michigan Law School; later still, he became Ford's first law partner in Grand Rapids. He limps from a childhood attack of polio; seated, he lifts the weak leg over the strong one to cross them. His rheumy eyes blink, and the muscles around them move with a remarkable rippling effect, under a thin slanting hedge of white eyebrows. When he speaks, it sounds as if he had BB shot rattling around in his larynx, and what he says is conservative, commonsensical, decent; the President listens to him. Something Phil Buchen has said to me one day, in talking about the coming to power of his friend, sticks in my mind as a kind of motto for the Administration: "This is not an era for change."

· · ·

9:35 A.M. The prebriefing session, with Nessen, Rumsfeld, Marsh, Hartmann, Friedersdorf.

NESSEN: Where do we go now, as far as legislative strategy on Cambodian aid is concerned?

FORD: Without knowing the details, I think we have to keep the pressure on. I strongly disagree with the position taken in the two Democratic caucuses. I hope that wiser heads will prevail in the end. . . .

Nessen tests the President on several other positions.

Suddenly there is a bad moment; it comes up from nowhere like a sudden whirling desert dust spout. Nessen has been reading from a newspaper column; "a White House source" has said something that Nessen says he thinks may need clarifying or correcting. The President seems to shrug it off.

RUMSFELD (*sharply*): Mr. President, I think you should read what it quotes Bob Hartmann as saying.

Nessen passes the clipping to Mr. Ford. He starts reading it. He does not light his pipe, does not lift his unlit pipe to his mouth. Hartmann's flushed face slowly turns to the right; his lips are pursed, and the habitual twinkle in his eye is replaced by something dangerous, something that can scratch; I remember that he is rather proud of having a paperweight of carborundum, which is used in abrading steel, on his desk. The President hands the clipping to Hartmann without comment. Hartmann glances at it.

HARTMANN: This is what we used to call in the trade "thumb-sucking." When a reporter doesn't have any facts, he sucks his thumb awhile and then he writes down whatever comes out of his thumb.

But Hartmann is crossing and recrossing his legs. Rumsfeld's eloquent hands have a delicate tremor. I watch the President closely, mindful of what he told me at breakfast yesterday: "It's more disturbing to me than anything. . . ."

This is where I really see the scope and influence of his self-control. I am so fascinated by his face, which is perfectly peaceful, perfectly serene, that I do not catch the exact words he speaks to Don Rumsfeld, but I cannot miss the equable, firm, unreproachful quality of his voice. Then:

FORD (*in silky tones*): Anything else, Ron?

NESSEN: What do I say about the conservatives who are calling Rockefeller a liability?

The nasty little twister has already passed; one can hardly believe it was ever there; the air is as still as glass. The next time Rumsfeld speaks, his voice is completely normal. Hartmann rubs the bag under his right eye with the back of his right hand, and when he takes his hand away the benign look has returned.

10:15 A.M. Nessen group out. Paperwork.

10:52 A.M. The President goes into the Cabinet Room to receive a delegation of Soviet officials, led by (it should not be incredible that stereotypes sometimes actually do show up) a simulacrum of a bear, a great hugger of a Russian man, State Minister of the Food Industry Voldemar Lein. With him are the ministers of food production, all looking well fed, for the Ukraine, Belorussia, Estonia, Armenia, Kazakhstan, Uzbekistan and the Russian Republic. These men have just completed a delicious tour. They have been invited by Donald M. Kendall, chairman of PepsiCo—which has established a bottling plant in the Soviet Union and distributes Soviet vodka here—to see how food is processed in the United States, and from sea to shining sea they have

visited plants of Hershey chocolate, Heinz soups and
canned foods, Sara Lee frozen cakes and pastries,
Kraftco cheese and margarine, Coors beer, Sun Maid
raisins, Roma wine, Valley Foundry (winery equip-
ment), Bird's Eye foods, Maxwell House coffee, Frito-
Lay potato products, Tropicana orange juice, Pepsi-
Cola bottling and Philip Morris cigarettes.

While waiting for the President, the various national
food ministers have been taking turns popping in and
out of the chair with the little brass plate on the back
which says THE PRESIDENT while a pal across the table
takes snapshots of them in the highest seat of power.
On the President's entrance everyone cools it and takes
a Cabinet member's chair.

Of all the establishments the Russians visited, the
one Minister Lein talks about with the most ursine joy
is Disney World.

FORD: Did you go in the Haunted House?

LEIN: (*rolling his eyes in terror*): *Da! Da! Da!*

The President makes a set speech, which is Russian-
ized by an American translator: ". . . helpful and bene-
ficial . . . General Secretary . . . Vladivostok . . . expan-
sion of trade . . . détente relationship. . . ."

Then Minister Lein makes a speech, which is Eng-
lished by a Soviet translator. Minister Lein, it seems, is
accustomed to good long feasts of talk. He does not
spare the courses. We learn a great deal from him
about food processing, as practiced both in the Union
of Soviet Socialist Republics and in the United States of
America. He grows expansive on the benefits of mutual
visitation, trade, friendship, cultural exchange and
détente.

Mr. Ford, maintaining firm eye contact even during
translational interludes, is growing larger and larger,

. . . *with Voldemar Lein*

his chin is jutting out farther and farther. At last the State Minister springs to his feet, and Mr. Ford springs to his feet. The State Minister snaps open a large suitcase of gifts—a huge buffalo carved from a root by a peasant, a scarf with ПЕПСИ-КОЛА (Pepsi-Cola) and МИР (peace) printed on it, an exquisite miniature samovar, a very large pipe, a cup and saucer, an ancient ruble and a bottle each of Ambassador and Stolichnaya vodka. By the time he gets around to mentioning the vodka, Minister Lein's arms, elbows bent, are flapping.

LEIN (*as translated*): When you are tired, President, drink a little from these two bottles and (*flap, flap*) you will be STRONG!

FORD (*elbows bent, but not quite flapping*): I WILL!

11:20 A.M. Secretary Schlesinger and General Scowcroft go into the Oval Office; I am not invited.

Once again, seeing Kissinger's deputy's back recede as the door closes, I begin thinking about what I have missed this week.

Why, I wonder, has this candid President opened the door so wide to me on domestic-policy meetings, and on appointments of all sorts, yet excluded me from every consideration of foreign affairs?

One answer, of course: Dr. Kissinger is away. Another: This has been a bad week—Cambodia, Vietnam, frustrations by the Congress.

But now I remember that when Mr. Ford first met with me a month ago to discuss this project, he told me (not then knowing that the Secretary would be in the Middle East this week), "The only meetings I can think of that you won't be able to sit in on are my talks with Henry." After that appointment Ron Nessen softened the blow of this exclusion by explaining to me that nobody, but nobody—excepting the Secretary's other self, Brent Scowcroft, and occasionally Secretary of Defense Schlesinger—goes in with Henry to discuss foreign policy with the President. General Scowcroft later confirmed this to me.

And now this idea suddenly bothers me, and even alarms me—not the idea of my own exile, I mean, but that United States foreign policy should be transacted man-to-man between Henry Kissinger and Gerald Ford. I have seen endless meetings of six, eight, ten advisers sitting with the President to hammer out policy on the economy and energy and Congressional tactics and everything else under the sun; there the President has heard numerous advisory voices. But foreign policy is apparently of a different order. Of course, Dr. Kissinger has the whole weight of the State Department behind him, and I am told that he does occasionally appear at senior staff meetings to brief the President's advisers; but in the formulation of settled policy, this President, who had a minimal exposure to foreign affairs before he came to office, hears, I am told, only one voice, and a mercurial voice it is, Henry Kissinger's. Yes, this is the most alarming thought I have had all week.

But that is not all there is to it. General Scowcroft is in there now with the Secretary of Defense; I can only speculate that they are discussing with the President the deteriorating military situation in Indochina. Earlier this morning General Scowcroft was in with David Peterson of the C.I.A. These couplings forcefully remind me of Dr. Kissinger's dual role—as Secretary of State and Assistant to the President on National Security Affairs.

General Scowcroft has told me that the National Security Council—which consists of the President, the Vice President, the Secretary of State and the Secretary of Defense, with the Director of the C.I.A. and the Chairman of the Joint Chiefs as attendant nonmembers—does not meet on a regular basis and does not set policy when it meets. Final policy, Scowcroft has told me, is set by the President in consultation with the council's chairman, who is Henry Kissinger.

Diplomacy, security, foreign intelligence—one daily voice for all? To advise a President with virtually no experience in those areas? Why are the President's domestic advisers, civilians, not present as a matter of course to speak for the citizenry on every occasion when foreign affairs and national security, with their horrendous potential for economic commitment and even armed conflict, are discussed?

Schlesinger and Scowcroft are in with the President for an hour and a half.

1:05 P.M. The Gridiron Club delegation, eight Grand Panjandrums of the Washington news corps, waits on the President with an invitation to their dinner. Photographs, standing with the President.

1:10 P.M. Winners of a White House Press Photographer's Contest in to stand beside the President and have their photographs photographed.

1:15 P.M. Lunch. That good old cottage cheese, drenched in that good old A-1 Sauce.

2:03 P.M. The no-more-spending meeting. Lynn, Seidman, Marsh, Hartmann, Buchen, Nessen, Scowcroft, Greenspan, Cannon, Friedersdorf, Cheney, O'Neill.

In his State-of-the-Union Message two months ago, the President said, "I have also concluded that no more spending programs can be initiated this year, except for energy. Further, I will not hesitate to veto any new spending programs adopted by the Congress." Aware, for some time, of all sorts of proposals, major and minor, some of them meritorious or even obligatory, that were "coming down the pike," James Lynn of the Office of Management and Budget has been trying to get a precise interpretation of these two sentences.

This is an uncomfortable meeting for the President, who finds himself on the spot for having given Congress a firm commitment which his advisers had obviously not thought through. He is pulled and pushed, in this discussion, by dissonant voices—humane, goading, "realistic."

Rumsfeld and Marsh

O'NEILL: If you go all the way with this, you're going to have to be against all kinds of things you may not want to be against—new medical devices, regulation of toxic substances. . . .

LYNN: Do you want to celebrate National Peanut Day?

GREENSPAN: The real problem is that there's no way, as an exact matter, to resolve this. . . . A substitute program isn't a "new" program. . . . Let's say that large spending programs are out, even if they have a future date on them—'77 or '78—but that you could get small programs under the tent. Of 1,000 programs, 950 would be small ones you don't care about. . . .

Ever since breakfast yesterday morning, I have been looking for signals of stress under the calm exterior. I have seen all week that it is not easy for Gerald Ford to be in the presence of contention; and that, by the

Greenspan, Buchen, Nessen, Scowcroft

Lynn, Seidman, O'Neill (seated)

same token, it is not easy for him to make what he refers to, in the language of umpires, as "a tough call." Yet once he has made such a decision, he does not agonize over it; rather, he becomes convinced of its rightness and is stubborn in its defense, even when, as with the Cambodian-aid request, it is unpopular, politically hopeless and of most improbable efficacy.

I am beginning to be able to tell when the pressure is on. He has three laughs: a radiant, healthy and catching outburst of real mirth; a hesitant laugh, expressing slight embarrassment or uncertainty; and, rarely, a mild, monosyllabic utterance of a manly giggle, delivered as the immediate preface to speech—which, when I have heard it, has seemed to cover flickering anger. Also, when he touches his face in one of two ways: thumb under chin, index and middle fingers up along the cheek, ring and little fingers bent down across the mouth; a grasping of chin between thumb and forefinger.

2:56 P.M. He returns to the Oval Office with General Scowcroft, who is in for twenty minutes.

3:16 P.M. A few spare minutes, time to rehearse alone a speech he must make during his next appointment.

4:00 P.M. Mr. Ford goes to the residence—first to the East Room, where he delivers the speech, which is pleasantly bantering, to 250 editors and publishers of small-town and rural weekly and daily newspapers, convened in Washington for the fourteenth annual Government Affairs Conference of the National Newspaper Association; and afterward to the State Dining Room, where drinks and a spread are furnished, and where he chats—he really does seem to enjoy these occasions—with some of the newspaper people and their families.

As he starts moving to leave, a moblet closes around him. He is besieged for autographs. The hallway is soon choked. He signs and signs, smiling and asking friendly questions. In a very few minutes, miraculously, he is swallowed by the elevator, off to the side of the cross hall.

"The secret in that kind of crowd," he says to me on the way back to the Oval Office, "is to keep your feet shuffling all the time. You get to your destination that way without offending anyone."

4:45 P.M. Personnel Director William N. Walker brings his staff of about a dozen into the Oval Office to meet the President. This is one small episode in Mr. Ford's obviously genuine drive toward accessibility and openness. He is charming to these staffers, each of whom, in his or her way, works hard for him.

I have an opportunity to ask him whether his accessibility, of which I have been a beneficiary, has drawbacks.

FORD: It does in some respects. Don Rumsfeld and I are trying to do something about it. I really should have more time during the day just to totally concentrate without listening. My tendency is to be more open. Don's tendency is, thank God, to start closing doors. We've made headway. I think after another few months we'll squeeze down the system, so to speak, so that I can have more time to actually think and contemplate. On the other hand—and I've argued this with Don—in many respects I think I'm a better listener than I am a reader. I have learned to read fast and to absorb, but there are certain things you can't do quickly, without talking them out—at least, I can't. I need more time. We have to find time to study, to think.

5:00 P.M. To the Cabinet Room, to meet with retiring Secretary of Labor Peter Brennan and a group of leaders of the building-trades unions, to talk about the lamentable rate of unemployment—almost 20 percent —among the members of some of those unions. These are big, hearty, tough men, and, as always, the President vibrates to strong chords that are struck near him. FORD: Pete . . . Like to welcome your colleagues . . . loyal, dedicated fellows. . . . What we've tried to do— we think it's a better way, though not necessarily for the building trades, I realize—is with a tax cut, if we could just get the Senators and Congressmen to move on it.
BRICKLAYERS' INTERNATIONAL PRESIDENT THOMAS F. MURPHY (*on the President's left, slamming the table with his hand*): Why don't you just send 'em home? FORD: Sometimes I wish I could, Tom.

Here, as I watch Mr. Ford gradually rise to the level of intensity and decibels of these former hodcarriers and masons and plasterers and bricklayers, I also see them quieted by his final imperturbability. Thus, I am aware of a principle of reciprocating influences always at work with this man. He yields, but only to a certain point; beyond that point, he tranquillizes.

5:56 P.M. Former Governor William Scranton of Pennsylvania, an old friend, into the Oval Office to talk. This is the only strong advisory voice Mr. Ford will have heard all week long expressing views even slightly

more liberal than his own. All the rest of his advice has come from people either as conservative as he, or more so.

6:24 P.M. Rumsfeld's deputy, Dick Cheney, and the Cabinet Secretary, Jim Connor, take the evening roundup today.

6:42 P.M. Paperwork.

7:11 P.M. The President emerges in his anteroom, ready to go home. But he is waylaid there by one of his military aides, who has been downstairs at a farewell party for General Lawson.

AIDE (*putting an arm around the President's shoulders*): Be a good guy, Mr. President, and listen to just one song from this Air Force bunch we've got down there.

The President is willing to be a good guy.

The aide runs off and soon reappears with a quartet

that calls itself The Winning Hand, belongs to the Arlington, Virginia, chapter of the Society for the Preservation and Encouragement of Barbershop Quartet Singing in America, and comes in several shapes and sizes of the same light-blue suit.

FORD (*pointing to Nell Yates, at the desk by the door to the Oval Office*): Sing a serenade to Nell there.

Out pops a pitch pipe. Then:

> *They say that it's a woman's world,*
>   *and I believe it's true.*
> *For women like to better men*
>   *in everything they do.*
> *In politics, science and industry,*
>   *the girls are always right.*
> *So I concede they're better than we —*
>   *they've earned the right to fight.*
> *And I'll be standing on the pier*
>   *handing out doughnuts*
> *When we send the girls*
>   *over there. . . .*

7:17 P.M. The President leaves for the residence, taking me with him.

We go up to the family quarters on the second floor, and he settles me in the "living room" and excuses himself; he says he wants to check in with Betty. He goes into the bedroom.

This "room" I am in is really just a grouping of furniture—a sofa covered in bright flowered cotton quilting, some easy chairs, a brass-railed oval coffee table, superb porcelain lamps, four fresh flower arrangements, no books lying around—at the end of the long, long second-floor central hall; it seems a cozy room with one wall missing.

After a few minutes the President emerges and says he'd like to have me come in and meet Betty.

The bedroom is a cheerful place; it is in the northwest corner of the mansion, and it must fill up to the brim with sunlight, as with sweet cider, in the daytime —though, come to think of it, there has not been a moment of sunshine all through this week of Mrs. Ford's having suffered with neck pain. She is in the wide bed. She looks frail. Her head rests on a small cylindrical pillow. I have an impression of a sea of whiteness and lace.

Susan is standing beyond the bed, in jeans and a Norwegian ski sweater.

Mrs. Ford raises her shoulders with difficulty to reach and shake my hand across the expanse of the bed. I am really glad to meet her; I have admired her straightforwardness and courage, and I have had a sense that just as Bess Truman stood close behind her Harry's backbone, so this woman fans up the warmth in her Jerry. She has been watching television. The President snaps off the set as we talk.

MRS. FORD (*to her husband*): Say! Lynda Bird Johnson Robb is writing a book, and she wants me to name the person I think is the most important American of all time. How about helping me?

The President seems about to make a suggestion, when she goes on:

MRS. FORD: I thought of Lincoln, and Jefferson, and of course old George—

SUSAN: What about Hamilton? Adams? John Hay?

MRS. FORD (*looking up at Susan*): No, I was thinking only of the top people—the giants. (*She turns her eyes —mischievous now—back to the President's.*) Would you buy Susan B. Anthony?

FORD (*with a peal of his good laugh*): There you go again!

The President, Susan and I are seated now in the living room. He is on his second Beefeater martini on the rocks. The delicate subject of intellectual competence has come up.

FORD: Well, you know, it's an interesting thing, John. I don't know whether grades are the way to say somebody is bright or dumb or otherwise. But I've often thought—when I was in high school, where the competition was mediocre, I got a little over a B average. When I went to Michigan, I did the same.[1] I think at law school—the same.

I said that Myres McDougal, a professor at the Yale Law School, had told me Mr. Ford had fared pretty

[1] In his four-year Michigan career, Mr. Ford earned A's in Decline of Rome to 1648, Civilization from 1648, Labor I and American Government. He received C's in English Composition I and II, second-year French, Finance, Geography, Money and Credit, History of the South Since 1860 and Psychology of Management. He got B's in everything else.

well there—had ranked about one-third of the way down from the top of his class.

FORD: Great guy. He was the Law School faculty member who was assigned to interview me as an applicant.[2] He—or somebody—told me that in the class I entered with, which had about 125, there were 98 or 99 who were college Phi Betes, of which I was not one. And they were extremely bright. Very able guys. . . . So I seem to have had a capability of competing with whatever competition there was at each level; and yet I could have enough outside activities to enjoy a broader spectrum of day-to-day living than some of them. But I must say I worked damn hard. And I happen to agree with people that grades are very important, but I don't think that's the final criterion by which to judge people.

SUSAN: Well, that's news!

FORD (*to Susan*): Yeah, I've been pushing you, beating you to get good grades, haven't I?

SUSAN: You put restrictions on, if my grades go down. . . .

We are at dinner. The table is lit by candles; dusk has fallen on the bold scenes from the Revolutionary War on the walls around us.

FORD: You watch, John. When they bring the dinner in, Susan's plate and mine will be all served—rations.

---

2 Professor McDougal's notes on that interview were: "Good-looking, well dressed, plenty of poise, personality excellent. Informational background none too good, but he is interested, mature and serious of purpose. Intelligence reasonably high. I should predict a 74 or 75 average with us. I see no reason for not taking him." The professor's academic prediction was remarkably accurate. Ford's average in all subjects was 74.8. He got 78 in Constitutional Law, 74 in Federal Jurisprudence, 79 in Public Control of Business.

But they'll pass things to you, and let you take as much as you want. You watch.

SUSAN: I've taken off thirty pounds.

The President's prediction is soon borne out.

Susan has been writing articles for *Seventeen*, and she and I talk awhile about Being Writers.

SUSAN: My second piece was about Mother's Day—really about the great job my mother has done all these years. Then they wanted me to do Father's Day for June. I said, "That's too much."

FORD: It's good discipline—writing for deadlines.

HERSEY: Yes.

SUSAN: The August issue is going into the works already. They want me to write about my summer. How do I know what my plans will be? . . .

Mr. Ford talks about clothes. He gets about three suits every two years, he says. The one he has on, he says, was made by Lloyd's, a tailor in Grand Rapids to whom he went for years—it is out of style, the lapel is too narrow, he points out. He can never throw anything out. The blue shirt he is wearing, he says, is new—just got it from a Washington tailor, Harvey Rosenthal. The President is now getting his suits from Rosenthal's, he says; they come into the White House for fittings. One of the luxuries . . .

We have butter-pecan ice cream for dessert. After it, Mr. Ford takes tea. He starts talking again about enjoying the Presidency:

FORD: I like meeting with one group to discuss this, and the next meeting to discuss that. I don't really object to anything unless it interferes with our family relationship. And that hasn't been too bad. Probably the major test was at Vail this Christmas, and it wasn't—

. . . I suppose somebody who is hypersensitive might say, "Gee, I couldn't do this, or that." But if you just relax and enjoy it, it doesn't make you tense, it doesn't make you irritable.

SUSAN: Just like when we were in Vail. Even though you did have the Cabinet meetings—when they were over, it was like you were back on your vacation.

FORD: It worked out very nicely.

SUSAN: Secretary Simon stayed, and we had a good time with him. He couldn't have been nicer.

FORD: The only thing that is disappointing—I guess any President has this. The President thinks he has the right answers. The facts of history are that he doesn't always—but he thinks he does. And he would like to implement, he'd like to execute—to get things done. But under our system, the Congress has a very definite partnership. Right now we are going through an extraordinary trauma in the relationship between the Congress and the President. I understand that. I've been on the other end of it. But if there was one part which I would really like to change, it would be the speed with which you could make decisions and carry them out—in foreign policy, particularly. . . .

We are in the family room now, he in his blue chair, I in the overstuffed chair next to it, and the time has come for me to ask him some direct questions.

Harry Truman seems to be much in his mind. What are the things he admires about him as President?

FORD: Well, he came from relatively humble beginnings. He obviously was a man who knew people, understood people and worked with people. He had a lot

of courage, was forthright, didn't hesitate to make decisions. Those are the things I admire.

What attributes does he feel he brings to the Presidency?

FORD: I don't like to talk about it. Maybe what I say is what I would like to have brought, but . . . I think I bring a responsible decision-making process, based on a great deal of fundamental knowledge of how things work in our Government. I consider myself very lucky that I bring this to the White House, that I have acquired, that I have retained, a great deal of background in the political process. I know I'm conscientious. I know I'm a person who can listen. I believe I bring out in people I work with their best qualities. I think I have a knack of picking people who have talent.

What would he like to be remembered for?

FORD: I think that America went through one of the most unbelievable periods in the last two or three years that we'd ever want to. And I found myself in a situation where somebody had to take over—internationally, domestically, governmentally—and handle circumstances such as had never transpired in this country before. And if I can be remembered for restoring public confidence in the Presidency, for handling all these transitional problems responsibly and effectively, for achieving decent results domestically as well as internationally, regardless of how long I serve, whether it's two and a half years or six and a half years, I think that's what I'd like on my tombstone.

•   •   •

He is restless. Maybe he is as dissatisfied with this last answer as I have been. He rings for a butler and asks for more tea for both of us.

Can he give, in a capsule, the essence of his political philosophy?

FORD: I happen to think that we should have great opportunity for people in this country to get ahead. Hard work should be rewarded. I don't think people who have had bad breaks should be penalized, but I don't think you can reward people who don't try.

Where does his conservatism come from?

FORD: I think it was the upbringing in my stepfather's family—he was a sort of a Horatio Alger in a limited sense. It was my upbringing in a family that had to live, not an austere, but a moderate life.

How conservative does he see himself as being?

FORD: Well, I'm conservative in that I believe in saving —I'm talking personally, now—I believe in saving, I believe in building through effort. On the other hand, I enjoy material things. This is a nice place to live, and there are many conveniences that are made available here. I enjoy belonging to Burning Tree. We were talking about clothes—I enjoy nice clothes, not flamboyant or extravagant. I enjoy doing nice things. But I enjoy these things because I worked for them.

Does he think that the material side of the Presidency, and its conveniences, won't get to him?

FORD: I don't think I've shown any evidence that they have, and I don't see why they should. I've had a long sixty years without any of this, so these aren't things that I couldn't get along without in the future.

What about the sense of power that comes with an office like this?

FORD: I don't enjoy it. I think I accept it as part of the responsibility. I recognize that it is there, and that I have to use it judiciously. I don't shy away from it.

Does he think of himself as a Middle American?

FORD: I do see myself as a Middle American. I have a Michigan background. I went to school in Michigan from kindergarten through college. But I've been fortunate enough to have exposures that broadened the spectrum, broadened the horizon.

How would he describe a Middle American?

FORD: A person who is moderate-to-conservative, philosophically; who yet has compassion for people less well-off than himself; who wants to have his country do what is right for everybody; who is concerned with the national security; who is willing to make sacrifices; who is willing to work; and who is a lot smarter than most politicians give him credit for being.

How can he use the word "compassion" so much— and ask for higher prices for food stamps?

FORD: The trouble with a lot of these programs, where compassion ought to be the main thrust, is that they get well beyond the properly intended scope. And the net result is that when you try to bring them back to focus on the people who need and deserve help— whether food stamps or welfare generally—when you try to cut out the undeserving so you can give more to the people who are really in need, you can't be compassionate for the ones who get cut out, because they shouldn't have been in the program in the first place. And yet they're the most vocal; they're the ones who feel that because they were on something, they ought to continue. Really, the ones that are deserving of compassion are the ones that complain the least. It's the ones who are sort of the fringe people who cause the most trouble and get the issue confused.

Perhaps I phrased that last question badly. I am thinking back to Tuesday, when I was first surprised by what seemed to me the hard sound in his voice, the sound of distance from ordinary people—which seemed so contradictory to the direct and unfeigned kindness he was able to offer whomever he met face to face. Perhaps I can come at this from another direction—by way of another contradiction in him.

He was famous in Congress for his gift of compromise, but even some of his good friends say he is stubborn at times. How do these two things go together?

FORD: It is paradoxical. I try to rationalize that when I am stubborn, I am right, and therefore compromise seems fundamentally wrong. Now I suppose to somebody who's sitting on the other side, when I take a firm position, he says, "Well, he's just being stubborn—not necessarily 100-percent right." But there are occasions where I will be very firm, and stubborn might be another term for it.

What are his feelings when he is criticized?

FORD: When I read or listen to criticism, I try to analyze whether it's legitimate by my standards; and if I think it's unfair and feel very secure in my judgment, sometimes I'm amused by the criticism, sometimes I'm irritated, but the last thing I'm going to do is let anyone know it. But as long as I feel that what I've done is right, I'm not going to be upset about it and fly off the handle or change my course of action. If the criticism is fair—and there are instances when I might have made a mistake—then I take it and look it over. If I've made a mistake, I don't hesitate to change.

Looking back, what mistakes?

FORD: Well, there's probably one incident in retrospect I might have handled differently, and this is the famous challenge to Bill Douglas. But at the time, I was faced with a very difficult practical problem within the Republican party in the House. Bill Douglas had made some decisions, and his married life was different than most—many conservative people were upset about him, and we had a very strong small group of very conservative Republicans in the Congress. And for a period of about a month or so, they kept telling me, "You either do something about it, or we're going to offer a motion of impeachment, which is a privileged motion of the highest, and we're going to force a vote." I tried to keep them from going off the deep end, and they kept pressuring and pressuring. And then this famous *Evergreen* publication came out, a very ill-advised article by the Justice in a magazine that I think is pornographic by any standards. And that upset me, plus the pressure from these others. So I said to myself, in order to keep the irresponsibles from forcing the vote, I will make this speech, and I will not say there should be impeachment, but that there ought to be a study. Well, I did it. I never demanded his impeachment. I advocated a study. Well, in retrospect, forgetting the pressures that were existent then, I suspect it was the one thing that was a bit out of character.

What does he say to those who call him a plodder and a man without charisma?

FORD: I kind of resent the word "plodder." (*What is it that one can hear in the careful way he says these words? There is something gathering, something clotting, under the perfect control.*) I would put it another way. I'm a determined person. And if I've got an objective, I'll make hours of sacrifice—whatever efforts are needed. Some people call it plodding. The word is somewhat downgraded, but I'd rather be a plodder and get someplace than have charisma and not make it.

Now I realize that we have shared a moment of strong and puzzling feelings. Beneath the control, I can hear that he is angry with me, and I am glad of it. He has a right to be angry; I have asked him hard questions, and just now an insulting one. For my part, although I am deeply troubled by some of his policies, and by the long reach and rigidity of his conservatism, I have nevertheless come to like him as a man—he has been most kind and generous with me; his good laugh, when I have heard it, has filled me with its energy and warmth. And so I am grateful for this human moment, even though it is ugly, for I feel that at last we have really and truly met.

But it is only a moment, as I must hurry on to the next question.

Does he have any chance to talk to poor people?

FORD: In this job, I have had very little. When I was in Congress, a great deal. When I was in Congress, I made a maximum effort. I think that was helpful, both substantively and politically.

Wouldn't it be now, too?

FORD: Well, we've thought about that, and quite frankly I've been intrigued with the program Giscard has, of having gone to dinner in the homes of citizens, or having people in. I'm a little hesitant about doing it, because it looks copycat. Now that I've talked about it, I think there's some merit in it. As to how you do it . . . I don't know if you've ever heard about my trailer operation.

What was that?

FORD: That was the smartest thing I ever did. Grand Rapids was the main area of the district. After I'd been in Congress about six years, I found I was spending 90 percent of my time in Grand Rapids, and not doing much out in the smaller communities in the rural areas. I got the idea of having Jerry Ford's Main Street Office. So we rented a trailer, and I would take it to Cedar Springs, and we'd advertise that I was going to be there in the morning. I'd speak, going to the high school and the grade school and talking to the kids, and then I'd speak at the Cedar Springs Rotary Club, or Kiwanis—this wasn't just campaign years, off-years as well. I'd walk up and down the main street for an hour or so, stopping at stores. And then from two thirty to eight o'clock I'd be in the trailer. And we would have anywhere from 25 to 125 people come and see me individually in the back room of the trailer. And I had my secretary or administrative assistant out front. In the course of two months in the fall, maybe three months, I'd do it in twenty-five, thirty different places. We would have anywhere from 1,500 to 2,000 people who would stop in and see me, to criticize, to compliment, to give us problems to work on. We could always say that I had my office within ten miles of every home in the district. People could never say they couldn't come and see me. It was the greatest political asset in a non-political way.

This picture excites me, and I interrupt him to exclaim how good it would be if he had a trailer like that now. I imagine the Presidential trailer in remote hamlets, on hot city streets. He is not interested in my enthusiasm, and at once I realize how silly it is—the mobs, security, a nation isn't a district. . . .

And yet, how good it would be if in some way he could speak—not just with Kissinger and Simon and Morton and Schlesinger, with Rumsfeld and Hartmann and Marsh and Buchen, with importunate politicians and selected intellectuals—but also, good listener that he is, inner mimic that he is, one-to-one with ordinary men and women, his constituents, from whom he has somehow drifted so far away.

FORD (*ignoring my interruption*): On some occasions I'd be in the trailer until midnight. It was interesting in that district. It had many strong, devout, Calvinistic Dutch people. Holland, Michigan. Zeeland, Michigan. In one area of the district, 90 percent of the people were strong Protestants—not Dutch Reform, but Dutch

Christian Reform, which is a group that broke off from Dutch Reform because it was too liberal. I would have the ministers from these areas in, and sit down with them before they'd talk about a problem, and they'd say, "Can we have a few moments of prayer?" And we'd pray in the trailer—sincerely, very devoutly.

Somehow, thinking about the trailer, I have lost the thread of all the hundreds of questions this week has raised in my mind. Thinking about more than the trailer, really. Thinking about what seemed for a moment possible but obviously is not; thinking about the insistent sound of caution in all that Mr. Ford has been saying this evening; thinking about the hopes that so many citizens have had for a whole new era, after the Nixon debacle, in our national way of looking at things —hopes for a time of change that is evidently not going to be fought for, or even dreamed of, by this man, because in his view, and in that of his advisers, "this is not an era for change."

The brown suitcase, full of papers, sits there like a reproach. I sense that the President is itching to get down to work. I thank him for dinner, and for his time, and for his openness. He considerately goes all the way downstairs in the elevator with me, to make sure I will find my way back to the West Wing, where I left my coat early this morning.

FORD: Good night, John. See you in the morning!

SATURDAY

The Shot Takes Off for Atlanta, Georgia

This morning he indulges in what he calls "sleeping over"; this means that he doesn't show up at the Oval Office until 8:30. He has a light schedule today—a chance to clear his desk.

8:34 A.M. Scowcroft and Peterson in. 8:55 A.M.—Peterson out. 9:35 A.M.—Scowcroft out, Marsh in. 9:50 A.M.—Marsh out.

The day has dawned with an overcast sky, but the forecast, at last, is excellent. Now suddenly a dollop of sunlight falls like a promise through a rip in the clouds and dilutes with finer stuff the artificial brilliance of the Oval Office. No more is needed to make the President ring for Terry O'Donnell and tell him to line up some golfing companions for the afternoon.

9:50 A.M. Cheney and Greenspan in. 10:15 A.M.—
Greenspan out. 10:25 A.M.—Cheney out. 11:00 A.M.
—Cheney in again. 11:35 A.M.—Cheney out again.
Paperwork.
GRANDFATHER SEYMOUR: Tock . . . Tock . . . Tock . . .

1:35 P.M. A motorcade of four cars leaves the South
Grounds: the President in a blue sedan, reading the
afternoon *Star-News* as he goes; a Secret Service car,
which follows the sedan closely; a staff car; a car for
the photographic pool, going along as far as the entrance gate to Burning Tree—just in case.

The President changes in the locker room, then goes
to the first tee, wearing now an old visored cap, brown-
on-brown saddled golf shoes, green pants and a blue
windbreaker of the Pinehurst Country Club, which he
picked up when he went there last year to visit the golf
Hall of Fame and played a round with the famed in-
ductees. With him are his good friend William Whyte,
a vice president and Washington lobbyist for United
States Steel; Clark MacGregor, once a fellow Congressman with Ford, later John Mitchell's successor as
Chairman of the Committee to Re-Elect the President
and now a Washington-based vice president of United
Aircraft Corp., and Webb Hayes, a Washington lawyer
and great-grandson of President Rutherford B. Hayes.

Ford teams up with Whyte; the foursome settles on a
"two-dollar Nassau"—a betting deal that can't hurt
anyone much. The men do not use golf carts; caddies
carry their clubs.

On the first few holes, the President has a bit of Oval
Office in his swing. His long game is very strong; his
chips and putts, more often than not, are too strong.
He putts with a wide stance suitable for good hard

clouts. The sun is fully out now. There is a breeze with sharp teeth that bite the flags on the greens. So discreet is Burning Tree Country Club that these flags don't even have numbers on them. One is conscious of several men, carrying odd-shaped cases, ranging in the woods on either side of the fairway and far ahead. Following the foursome at a polite distance are Dick Keiser, Chief of the Presidential Protective Division of the Secret Service, who is often taken for the President in crowds; Lieutenant Commander Stephen Todd, the President's naval aide, carrying a walkie-talkie, to be in touch with the White House communications center at all times; and Dr. Lukash.

It is the seventh hole, par four.

Gerald Ford's huge tee shot takes off for Atlanta, Georgia, but the ball has a mind of its own and in midair veers left toward Charleston, South Carolina; on the way there, however, it hits a tall tree and, with distinctly Presidential luck, bounces out to a splendid lie in the left rough.

There, with a No. 2 wood, the President connects so hard that one is forced to wonder what that small sphere stands for in his mind. The ball rises and rises and flies as straight and true as Air Force One nonstop to the green, to within ten feet of the pin.

The President cups his hands around his mouth and exultantly shouts to his partner across the fairway: "Hey, Bill, is that where I'm supposed to put it?"

APPENDIX

The following members of the Ford Administration figured in the described events of March 10–16, 1975; they are identified with the posts they held at that time.

PETER BRENNAN, Secretary of Labor

PHILIP W. BUCHEN, Counsel to the President

DR. ARTHUR F. BURNS, Chairman, Federal Reserve Board

EARL L. BUTZ, Secretary of Agriculture

JAMES M. CANNON, Assistant to the President for
  Domestic Affairs; Executive Director, Domestic Council

JOHN J. CASSERLY, Speechwriter

RICHARD B. CHENEY, Deputy Assistant to the President

WILLIAM T. COLEMAN, Secretary of Transportation

JAMES CONNOR, Cabinet Secretary

APPENDIX

MILTON A. FRIEDMAN, Deputy Editor, Editorial Office

MAX L. FRIEDERSDORF, Assistant to the President for Legislative Affairs

DR. ROBERT GOLDWIN, Consultant, Liaison with Academics

ALAN GREENSPAN, Chairman, Council of Economic Advisers

ROBERT T. HARTMANN, Counsellor to the President

CARLA A. HILLS, Secretary of Housing and Urban Development

JOHN W. HUSHEN, Deputy Press Secretary to the President

DAVID H. KENNERLY, Personal Photographer to the President

DR. HENRY A. KISSINGER, Secretary of State; Assistant to the President for National Security Affairs; Chairman, National Security Council

REAR ADMIRAL WILLIAM M. LUKASH, MC, USN, Physician to the President

JAMES T. LYNN, Assistant to the President for Management and Budget; Director, Office of Management and Budget

JOHN O. MARSH, JR., Counsellor to the President

ROGERS C. B. MORTON, Secretary of the Interior

RONALD H. NESSEN, Press Secretary to the President

TERENCE O'DONNELL, Aide to the President

PAUL H. O'NEILL, Deputy Director, Office of Management and Budget

ROBERT ORBEN, Consultant, Speechwriting

DAVID PETERSON, White House Support Staff, C.I.A.

NELSON ROCKEFELLER, Vice President

DONALD N. RUMSFELD, Assistant to the President

JAMES R. SCHLESINGER, Secretary of Defense

LIEUTENANT GENERAL BRENT SCOWCROFT, USAF, Deputy Assistant to the President for National Security Affairs

L. WILLIAM SEIDMAN, Assistant to the President for Economic Affairs

WILLIAM E. SIMON, Secretary of the Treasury

PAUL A. THEIS, Executive Editor, Editorial Office

RUSSELL E. TRAIN, Administrator, Environmental
Protection Agency

WILLIAM N. WALKER, Director, Presidential Personnel
Office

CASPAR WEINBERGER, Secretary of Health, Education, and
Welfare

FRANK ZARB, Administrator, Federal Energy Agency

A NOTE ABOUT THE AUTHOR

John Hersey was born in Tientsin, China, in 1914, and lived there until 1925, when his family returned to the United States. He studied at Yale and at Clare College, Cambridge University. After serving for several months as secretary to Sinclair Lewis, he worked as a journalist and war correspondent. Since 1947 he has devoted his time mainly to fiction. He has won the Pulitzer Prize and is a member of the American Academy of Arts and Letters. From 1965 to 1970 he was Master of Pierson College at Yale, and he spent the following year as Writer-in-Residence at the American Academy in Rome. He now lives in New Haven, Connecticut, and teaches at Yale.

A NOTE ON THE TYPE

This book was set on the Linotype in a face called Primer, designed by Rudolph Ruzicka, who was earlier responsible for the design of Fairfield and Fairfield Medium, Linotype faces whose virtues have for some time been accorded wide recognition.

The complete range of sizes of Primer was first made available in 1954, although the pilot size of 12-point was ready as early as 1951. The design of the face makes general reference to Linotype Century—long a serviceable type, totally lacking in manner or frills of any kind—but brilliantly corrects its characterless quality.

The book was composed, printed, and bound by American Book–Stratford Press, Saddlebrook, New Jersey.

Design by Christine Aulicino.